THE WAR IN AFRICA
AND THE FAR EAST,
1914–17

German soldiers arrive in German South-West Africa in 1902. (*Library of Congress*)

The War in Africa and the Far East, 1914–17

Herbert Charles O'Neill

WESTHOLME
Yardley

Westholme Publishing, LLC
904 Edgewood Road
Yardley, Pennsylvania 19067
Visit our Web site at www.westholmepublishing.com

First Printing
10 9 8 7 6 5 4 3 2 1
ISBN: 978-1-59416-068-4
Also available as an eBook

Printed in United States of America.

CONTENTS

List of Maps

Foreword

There are already a number of excellent books dealing with various phases of the campaign in the German Colonies; but so far no one has attempted to present a picture of all the campaigns. The present book has been written to meet this need, and, in spite of its shortness, I hope that it gives a clear outline of the military operations which led to the occupation of the whole of Germany's Colonial Empire. I have spared no pains to ensure the accuracy of the facts, and in the maps I have attempted to supplement and sum up the narrative by tracing the main lines of the various columns. The material I have used includes almost every book that has so far appeared; but the groundwork was furnished by the official dispatches.

In such a compass it has been impossible to do perfect justice to the splendid behaviour of the troops, both white and native, who carried out these arduous campaigns; and perhaps the human figures show up a little shadowy. But my aim has been chiefly to make clear the military problem and the operations which led to its solution; and I think that if these are grasped the human side will sufficiently appear.

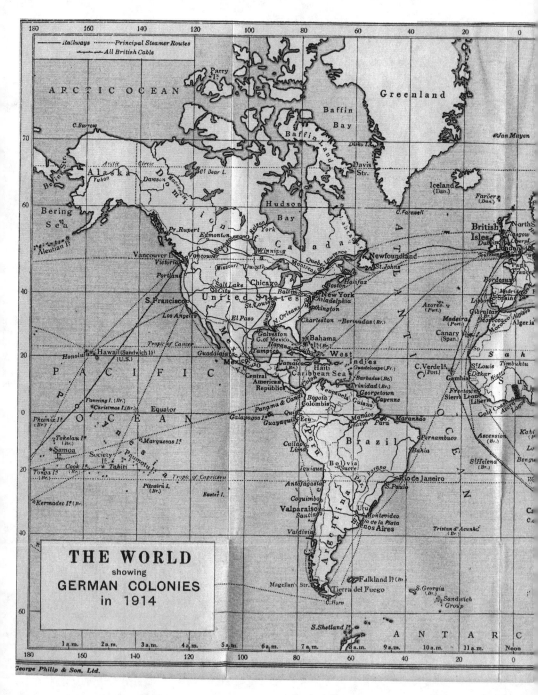

THE WORLD
showing
GERMAN COLONIES
in 1914

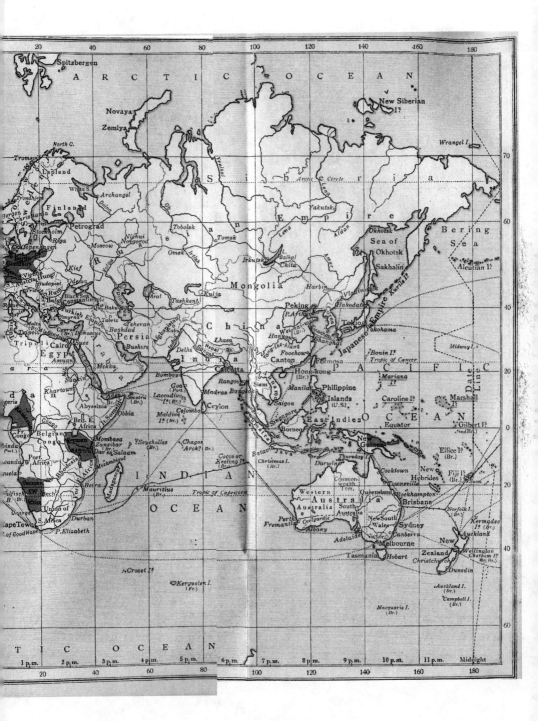

A German poster depicting Britain as a spider, Germany as an eagle sitting overhead, and Uncle Sam and two others tied up in a web in the background. *L´ Entente Cordiale* was a diplomatic agreement signed in 1904 by France and Great Britain which adjusted the colonial disputes between the two countries, and paved the way for Anglo-French cooperation against German expansion in Europe and in the colonial world. (*Library of Congress*)

THE FOUNDATIONS OF WORLD POWER

WHEN THE WAR BROKE OUT the German flag flew over a fairly compact group of settlements in the Pacific and a number of great colonies in Africa. But the German colonies were not like those of other nations. The vast majority of colonies came to their parent countries by a sort of natural accretion. Men were driven by the imperious thirst for adventure to travel far from their native lands into the unknown. When they reached habitable lands they made the fact known, and soon a stream of settlers and traders followed in their wake. In such wise the parent countries came to find their interests spread abroad and their settlements were proportionate to their liking for seafaring.

The German colonies were acquired very differently, and their history is directly traceable to the difference. Germany about a quarter of a century ago [1884] suddenly awoke to the fact that she had no colonies, and that other nations had them. They were therefore desirable. Accordingly, in a cautious and deliberate way, she set herself to obtain colonies. Her lack of success in colonial speculation is due to this inversion of normal expansion; for her colonists did not so much choose the lands as accept territories already chosen by their Government.

Each of three chief African colonies [Togoland, Kamerun, German East Africa] had been refused by Britain, which was as reluctant to undertake the responsibility of new administrative areas as Germany was anxious to have them. Their role was, then, different in Germany. Whereas other countries derived advantage from their colonies incidentally, Germany sought promising colonies specifically for what they might earn. The German colonies were, moreover, parts of her armaments—far-flung sensitive tentacles which could register and report to the central Government at Berlin, and act as cover and feeder for her armed units. When Germany's ambitions for sea-power gathered definition, the colonies were part of the framework upon which her schemes depended. If they could have been preserved intact, the Allies' control of the seas would never have been more than a fiction. German ships would have been able to coal and supply there, and from these bases raid the Allied transport continually.

Even if the Germans had prevailed upon the Allies to regard the African colonies as neutral, they would still have been able to inform their ships of the neighbourhood of cruisers, and so would have made the task of searching for German shipping much more difficult. And there can be little doubt that neutrality would have been used merely as a cloak to cover their attempts to raise native Africa against the Allies. Moreover, since the Germans were bound to lose their colonies if they were to be thrown open to attack, and the Allies would have this counterbalance to possible enemy gains in Europe, it was clearly to their advantage to have as many of the colonies as possible declared neutral.

Hence we find the Governor of Togoland, acting on instructions from Berlin, proposing to the British and French Governors of the adjacent colonies that these colonies should be treated as neutral. The pretext was the undesirableness of a conflict between the white rulers. But as there can be no doubt what would have happened if the Germans had been in the majority in Africa, the proposal was brushed aside.

For the neutrality of Kamerun and German East Africa there was a more colourable pretext. The Berlin Conference of 1884–5 had included a declaration favouring but not deciding the neutrality of the basin of the Congo, and interpreting it to cover nearly a third of Kamerun, the whole of German East Africa, nearly half of French Equatorial Africa, British East Africa, Uganda, Nyassaland, part of Rhodesia, and the northern part of Portuguese East Africa. On August 23rd (1914) the German Under-Secretary for Foreign Affairs opened negotiations through the American Ambassador in Berlin, Mr. James W. Gerard, to obtain the neutralisation of this area. The United States Government forwarded the suggestion without comment, and it was at once refused.

Britain and France had already been approached by the Belgian Minister for Foreign Affairs as to their intentions, and at first France seemed inclined to agree to a proclamation of neutrality. But on August 17th M. Davignon was informed by the Belgian Minister in London that both the British and the French had decided not to accept a state which would chiefly operate against them. Germany would have secured the most vulnerable part of Kamerun and could thenceforward attack the colonies north and south with impunity; and Germany would have prevented the Allies obtaining a considerable counterbalance to her conquests in Europe.

The behaviour of Belgium in Africa had been as correct as in Europe. The Congo Free State was the only declared neutral territory, and although Belgium was invaded and her neutrality violated, the Governor-General of the Belgian Congo had been instructed to observe a purely defensive attitude. The Belgian port Lukuga on Lake Tanganyika was bombarded on August 22nd by the Germans, and thus, when they were seeking to impose neutrality on the Allies, they had already delivered an attack on the territory of the Belgian Congo. Even then the Belgians did not retaliate. Only on August 28th was the Governor-General empowered to help the French, since German columns in Kamerun were threatening the Congo basin. Two days later Belgian help was sought by and given to the French.

The German colonies therefore became the scenes of active warfare, and one by one passed to the Allies. After the first two months the German flag was to be found, outside Europe, in Africa alone. By the end of the second year of the war it was to be found only in German East Africa. At the end of the year 1917 the last of the German colonies was completely occupied by the Allies.

If there had been no war in Europe to overshadow the campaigns in the colonies the world would have been thrilled by these struggles which epitomised centuries of warfare. The most modern equipment of scientific warfare was to be found side by side with the arms and framework of war whose memory is preserved only in forgotten textbooks. Dense thickets of jungle, vast stretches of waterless country, fever-ridden swamps, wild animals, and even wild bees were often more formidable obstacles to the Allies than any resistance of the enemy.

The campaigns were generally made up of numerous small struggles, in which a handful of men fought at times for days against a superior enemy and beat him off when they had reached the limit of their resources. Each of these episodes is worthy of record, and the series forms a fitting pendant to the romance of the exploration and discovery of the country in which it has its setting.

For the present the story can only be told in outline with a little of the incident that makes the conquest of Germany's colonies rank among the most stirring exploits of history.

General view of Lome, Togoland, before World War I. (*Wire Service*)

2

THE CAMPAIGN IN TOGOLAND

T HE CAMPAIGN IN TOGOLAND WAS begun and rounded off in the first month of the war. The colony is a little larger than Ireland in area, though it has a coastline of only 32 miles; and it forms a sort of island in Allied territory. To the west lies the British Gold Coast colony, to the north and east the French territories of Upper Senegal and Dahomey. Its resources had been considerably developed by Germany, but its main importance was the high-power wireless station which had been erected secretly at Kamina. From Kamina it was possible to transmit messages direct to Berlin, and the importance of retaining the use of so powerful an installation is obvious. It was this consideration which moved the German Government, through Major Hans-Georg von Döring, Acting Governor and Commanding Officer in Togoland, to propose on August 4th and 5th 1914 that the colony and the settlements which hemmed it in should remain neutral.

But the suggestion, like the proposal of a wider neutrality, was, as we have seen, brushed aside, and French colonial troops entered the colony from the east on the 6th as Captain Barker was approaching Lome, the chief port and capital, from the west. Captain Barker demanded the surrender of Togoland, but when he returned at the expiration of the armistice on the 7th, Lome was found to have been evacuated, and the French had taken Anecho and Togo. The District Commissioner informed Captain Barker that the colony was surrendered up to a line 120 kilometres (almost 75 miles) north of the capital.

The only possible justification of further resistance rested on the assumption that the war would be ended within a short period. By falling back to within about 30 miles of Kamina the Germans circumscribed the problem of defence, and von Doling was urged in four different communications to hold the wireless station. But with columns converging upon it from every direction its fall could only be a matter of time, and even of a short time.

The French and the British agreed to operate together under the command of Colonel Bryant, who landed at Lome on August 12th, with two companies of the Gold Coast Regiment—some 600 men, including 57 Europeans, with 2,000 native carriers. The main force at once pushed up the railway towards Kamina and achieved contact with the enemy, about the same time that Captain Potter cut off part of von Döring's force, which was endeavouring to join the main body of the enemy. A little later Captain Castaing, of the French Colonial Infantry, joined Colonel Bryant, and on August 20th the Allied force reached Nuatja. Two days afterwards a fierce engagement took place. At Chra, where the river of the same name crosses the railway, the Germans lay carefully entrenched. They had blown up the bridge over the river and had taken up a position on the northern bank covered by dense bush. The opposing forces were, roughly, equal—about 60 or 70 Europeans and 400 natives. But the enemy position was extremely strong, and after struggling

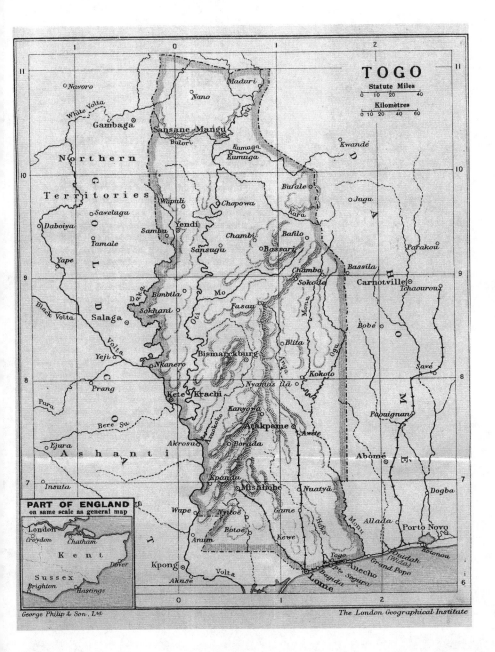

TOGO

German prisoners captured in Togoland are marched into Freetown, Sierra Leone, on February 1, 1915. The British Sierre Leone Company established Freetown in 1792. Sierre Leone became an independent country in 1961. (*Illustrated War News*)

throughout the day the Germans were still on the ground. They had lost very little, though the Allies suffered casualties. But the German commander learned that the French commander in Dahomey was advancing on Kamina, in his rear, and he evacuated the position on the Chra during the night.

There was no more fighting. On the night of August 24th loud explosions were heard from the direction of Kamina, and the conspicuous wireless apparatus disappeared. The Germans were preparing to surrender. Negotiations were opened by Major von Röben on the 25th, but he was informed that no terms could be accepted. On the following day the Germans agreed to surrender unconditionally.

The northern end of the colony had been already overrun by the Allies. The campaign was one of long marches on poor rations. But there was little resistance, and desertions from the enemy were frequent.

With the surrender of Kamina the colony passed to the Allies. It had been conquered in three weeks; and within three months the administration had been sufficiently reorganised to permit the colony to undertake trade with the Allies, as smoothly as if it had always belonged to them.

The preference of the native for British and French rule, which was so conspicuously shown in the other African campaigns, was manifested strikingly in Togoland, and was of the greatest help in the re-establishment of order.

German troops assigned to the defense of Tsing-Tau, Kiao-Chau, China, photographed in 1914. (*Library of Congress*)

3

The Pacific Colonies

The German colonies in the Pacific, though not very extensive, were extremely important links in the German scheme of world-policy. If we view the Pacific as an ocean basin lying between the land masses of America and the western coasts of Asia, we can see at once the deliberateness with which these colonies had been acquired. Their centre of gravity looks to the west, to Asia, and particularly, we may infer, to China and to India.

The largest of the Pacific colonies was the northeastern part of New Guinea, which comprised some 70,000 square miles, and was known as Kaiser Wilhelm Land. From Friedrich Wilhelmshafen and Constantinhafen, the chief ports, it exported some rubber and a considerable amount of copra and cocoa. The New Guinea Protectorate also included a number of neighbouring islands, and had its administrative centre at Rabaul in New Pomerania. This island, which had two good ports—Herbertshohe and Simpsonshafen (the port of Rabaul)—was one of the Bismarck Archipelago, which included New Mecklenburg, New Hanover, Admiralty Island, and New Lauenburg, with about 200 other tiny

Top, German officer posing with police recruits at Friedrich-Wilhelmshafen, New Guinea. Germany began occupying a portion of New Guinea in 1884. Bottom, German soldiers in Palau. Although claimed by Spain, Germany occupied the island in 1895 and eventually purchased the colonial rights following Spain's defeat in the Spanish-American War. (*Deutsche Kolonialgesellschaff Bibliothek*)

islands. To the east lay the two islands of the Solomon group, Bougainville and Buka, which belonged to Germany.

North of the Equator, but forming part of the same protectorate, were the Mariana or Ladrone Islands, the Eastern and Western Carolines, and the Marshall Islands, some distance to the east.

HMAS *Australia*, an Indefatigable class battlecruiser, was commissioned in July 1913 and became the Australian flagship. Her sister ship, *Indefatigable* was destroyed during the Battle of Jutland in May 1916. (*Wire Service*)

These groups included hundreds of coral islands of little value, producing some copra and phosphates. The detached island Nauru and the Samoa Islands, which lay far to the east like a sentinel outpost, completed the list of Germany's Pacific possessions, except for Kiao-Chau on the mainland. Taken together, they formed a fairly wide and organised sphere of influence.

These colonies were all nerve centres, presenting their impressions to the central brain at Berlin. Armed with high-power wireless installations, they could inform Germany's fugitive naval vessels of all that happened from India to America, and through Africa could communicate with Berlin. They afforded a potential harbourage for all German shipping and could circumvent the plans of the Allied navies.

The speed and completeness with which the German Pacific colonies were occupied and rendered harmless form one of the finest achievements of the Allies. Samoa was the first to fall. The principal islands of the group, which had been ceded to Germany by an agreement with Great Britain and America in 1899, were occupied by a New Zealand contingent without opposition. The expedition set out on August 15th from Wellington, accompanied by the British cruisers *Psyche*, *Pyramus*, and *Philomel*, and steamed first for New Caledonia to avoid the German cruisers *Scharnhorst* and *Gneisenau*. After three days' interval it left, on August 23rd, with an additional cruiser, the French vessel *Montcalm*, and was joined by the Australian battle-cruiser *Australia* and the cruiser *Melbourne*. Rear-Admiral Sir George Patey, on the *Australia*, now took charge. A call was made at Fiji, and then the expedition steamed for Samoa.

Rear-Admiral Sir George Edwin Patey (d. 1935), commander-in-chief of the Australian Squadron. Following the Allied occupation of German New Guinea, Patey led his squadron in pursuit of the German cruisers *Scharnhorst* and *Gneisenau*, which were both destroyed by a British task force at the Battle of the Falkland Islands in December 1914.

It lay off the coast of Upolu Island on August 30th, and after the harbour had been swept for mines the *Psyche* steamed in to Apia, the seat of the Government, and demanded the surrender of the island. Taken by surprise and unable to meet the force against them, the Germans yielded, the vessels entered the harbour, bluejackets landed and seized the Custom House, streets, and bridges, while the expeditionary force was landing. The German flag was hauled down, and the British flag was hoisted to a royal salute from the warships, next morning.

The Australian Government showed a notable disinterestedness in thus putting its navy at the services of the sister Dominion of New Zealand before proceeding to carry out its own plans. All the remaining German possessions in the South Pacific were taken by Australia, and with considerable dispatch.

New Pomerania was first reconnoitred, Rear-Admiral Sir George Patey being again in charge of the expedition. The British flag was

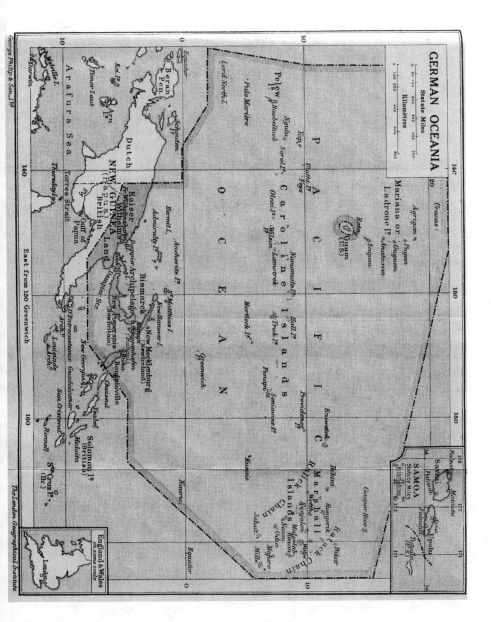

hoisted on September 11th at Herbertshohe without opposition. Simpsonshafen and Rabaul were also occupied without trouble; but Commander J. A. H. Beresford, who had landed at dawn on the 11th to capture the wireless station, had to fight through nearly four miles of bush. Mines had been laid across the road, men had been stationed in rifle posts, and there were snipers hidden in the tops of palms. After eighteen hours' fighting, the German force was defeated and the wireless station was captured at 1:00 A.M. on September 12th. A base was promptly established at Simpsonshafen, and garrisons were left at Rabaul and Herbertshohe.

Two days later the German Solomon Islands were surrendered without opposition. Kaiser Wilhelm Land also gave in without a struggle. A graver resistance had been expected there; but the Germans seem to have concentrated their small force for the defence of the wireless station at Herbertshohe. In less than a fortnight the bulk of Germany's southern Pacific possessions had surrendered. Nauru was handed over on November 6th.

MEANWHILE THE GERMAN POSSESSIONS in the northern Pacific had fallen to Britain's ally, Japan. Summoned at the outbreak of war under the terms of alliance, Japan had loyally stood by her bond, and in a carefully worded document "advised" Germany to withdraw her warships and hand over the colony of Kiao-Chau. The "advice" was tendered in the same tone and in almost the same language as that in which, at the instigation of Germany, Japan had been "advised" by Russia to abandon Port Arthur in 1895. The ultimatum was delivered on August 15th, and expired at noon on August 23rd. The Japanese Ambassador in Berlin was informed that there was no reply, and Japan declared war, and with the least possible delay set about the capture of Kiao-Chau and the Mariana,

A view of Tsing-Tau on the eve of World War I. Tsing-Tau was the main port of Germany's Kiao-Chau colony from 1898 to 1914. (*Wire Service*)

Caroline and Marshall Islands. The three groups were in the hands of Japan by the end of the first week of October, and they were promptly handed over to Australia. With them fell the powerful wireless station at Yap (Carolines), and another link of Germany's world empire was broken.

The Capture of Kiao-Chau

The sole instance of success in German colonial administration was the leased territory about the Bay of Kiao-Chau. The bay itself was a splendid harbour, with a narrow mouth. On the tongue of land which bounded it towards the east lay the Port of Tsing-Tau, upon which Germany had lavished so much careful forethought. It was organised admirably. Schools were founded; broad streets were laid out; splendid buildings were erected; there were well-planned and carefully-tended gardens; the harbour was provided with building slips; a railway was made, and the trade of the province was shepherded along it to the port. It was, as Bülow said, a centre whence

German Third Sea Battalion troops manning an automatic gun in the Tsing-Tau defenses. They are wearing the shakos with covers issued to machine gun units and mountain troops. The black bands were typically associated with manouvers but may have, in this case, distinguished the naval troops from those of the regular army. (*Illustrated War News*)

Germany could wield "a decisive influence on the future of the Far East."

In August, 1914, there lay in the harbour a formidable German naval squadron, and the territory provided the Germans with an excellent base for operations against the Imperial communications. The colony was defended by from 5,000 to 6,000 men, including machine gun sections, garrison and marine artillery. The Governor, Admiral Meyer-Waldeck, was ordered to resist to the last, and Tsing-Tau was well protected from the land side and turned only one face to the sea. The Germans were amply furnished with mines, and used them in great numbers.

The Japanese force comprised some 22,980 officers and men under General Kamio, a specially planned siege army with numbers of guns of calibres up to 11-inch; and it was assisted by a battal-

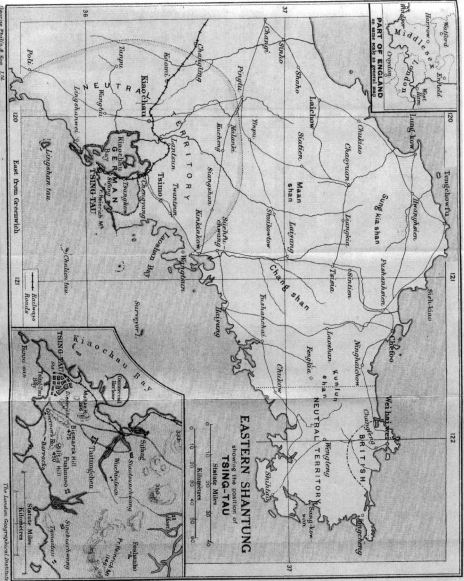

EASTERN SHANTUNG
showing the position of
TSING-TAU

ion of South Wales Borderers and about
half a battalion of 36th Sikhs under
General Barnardiston. The plan of the
campaign was to invest Tsing-Tau by
drawing a line across the peninsula on
which it stood, and then to reduce it
methodically; but it was necessary also
to occupy the whole territory over
which Germany exercised her influence and to take over the German line
which ran to Tsinan-fu.

Admiral Alfred William Moritz
Meyer-Waldeck (1864–1928),
governor of Kiao-Chau. (*Wire
Service*)

On August 27th a number of islands
lying about the mouth of the bay were
seized for use as a base, and mine-
sweeping operations were begun. A
week later, troops were landed at Lung-
Kow, in Chinese territory, the protest of China being met by the
rejoinder that in allowing Kiao-Chau to become a centre for military operations she had already permitted the violation of her neutrality. This force was to cut off the German territory from the
Chinese hinterland; and in ten days it had seized the station at
Kiao-Chau, which lies some three miles from the western shore of
the bay.

A period of torrential rains set in, and the floods imposed an
effective check upon active operations. But the main Japanese force
and the British contingent were landed without difficulty in
Laoshan Bay to the north of Tsing-Tau, and the days were filled
with Japanese aeroplane raids and a desultory bombardment on
both sides. The Japanese airmen achieved considerable success; but
the Germans, who attempted at night to retort by bombing the
Japanese squadron and the British ships under Vice-Admiral Kato,

Japanese artillerymen awaiting telephone orders from Headquarters before starting the bombardment of Tsing-Tau. Assisted by Allied warships, the Japanese batteries pounded the German defensive positions around the fortified city. (*Illustrated War News*)

found that the naval vessels had mysteriously changed their moorings during the darkness.

The floods had subsided to some extent by September 25th, and the Japanese began to move inland. On the following day, marching westward, they occupied the village of Tsimo, and continued their progress during the last days of the month against considerable resistance. Their right flank was bombarded by the German ships which Admiral von Spee had left after taking his main squadron out before the expiry of the ultimatum. But the Japanese suffered little damage, the aeroplanes forcing the warships to draw off. After three days' fighting the Allies were within five miles of Tsing-Tau, and they there met and defeated a heavy German counter-attack, assisted by aeroplanes and warships, on the last day of the month. On October 1st the fortress was completely invested on the land side, and the first stage of the land operations was complete.

Japanese officers looking carefully at the first British troops deployed to begin the joint assault on Tsing-Tau. The British and East Indian soldiers landed in Lao-shan Bay on September 24, 1914. (*Illustrated War News*)

Meanwhile, the Japanese were occupying the territory, farther inland, which had come under German influence, and by October 3rd they had taken possession of the railway from Tsinan-fu. Five days later General Kamio seized Prince Heinrich Hill, a position commanding the Tsing-Tau positions, and was surprised to find so little effective resistance. He now began to get his siege artillery in position—a very difficult operation in the sodden state of the ground; and, expecting a prolonged struggle for the fortress, gave a safe conduct through the Allied lines to European ladies and children with the American Ambassador. Sapping was pressed forward, and on the last day of the month the Allies opened a prolonged bombardment by land and sea. It was the Emperor's birthday, and the Japanese celebrated it by beating the fortifications to dust.

The main defensive works lay on the hills Moltke, Bismarck, and Iltis, which formed a line slightly to the north-east of the port. In advance of them were powerfully constructed redoubts, the approaches to which were prepared in the most scientific way. Over

Japanese troops inspecting the wide barbed wire obstacles surrounding Tsing-Tau. During the final assault on Tsing-Tau the Japanese had 14 officers wounded and 426 men killed. (*Illustrated War News*)

a mile or so of ground had been sown with obstacles. There was a dense mass of barbed wire, twisted about and firmly held in place by stakes. Then came a gentle slope, an almost perfect field of fire, without a vestige of cover. Each space would have to be carried without the help of the Allied guns, which could only interpose a curtain of fire beyond. These positions forced, an almost identical series lay beyond before the troops could reach the machine-guns, mortars, and rifles that awaited them in the redoubts. Shrapnel bursting from the forts would have made such ground almost impassable, and hence the fortified hills had to be made powerless before the infantry could have a chance of success.

On November 1st H.M.S. *Triumph* is said to have achieved a record by putting out of action the forts on Bismarck Hill with seven shots; and, with this achievement, only two forts were left sufficiently intact to keep up their answering cannonade. The dockyards were on fire; the oil tanks sent up a thick black smoke shot with flames that gleamed oddly in the night. When the fortress was

Two German coastal guns completely upended by direct hits from Japanese naval artillery during their intensive bombardment of Tsing-Tau. (*Illustrated War News*)

entered later it was seen how extraordinarily accurate the firing had been. Many of the forts were mere heaps of debris; and some were burnt out. Under cover of the bombardment, the troops went forward, and on November 3rd had seized part of the approaches to the redoubts with 800 prisoners.

Three days later the final assault was being approached. The troops were near to the German lines. During the night the line of redoubts was captured with small forces. On the right wing the British and Japanese captured the first redoubt; the two works in the centre were taken by four companies of Japanese sappers under General Yamada, and the two on the left fell to an attack of about the same dimensions under General Horiuchi.

There still lay over half a mile of dead ground, sown with obstacles, before the steep slopes to the Moltke, Bismarck, and Iltis hills were reached. But by 6:30 A.M. small bodies of skirmishers had surmounted these obstacles, and the troops lay waiting, tense and ready, for the final assault *en masse*. This was never to take place. As the morning light broke white flags were seen to be fluttering from the buildings of the town. The fortress had capitulated. Its fate was sealed as soon as Japan declared war; but it had been thought that the Germans would obey their Kaiser's order and hold out to the last. There seemed to the Japanese a savour of dishonour in the surrender, and this feeling was expressed in a statement published in Tokio, sarcastically applauding "the *wisdom* of the garrison." Germany won no laurels in the East.

IN THREE MONTHS THE GERMAN FLAG HAD BEEN swept from the Pacific. On land it had no longer a foothold there, and its fugitive appearance at sea was nearing its end. The colonies which Germany had purchased, leased, or taken in the Pacific were no more, Kiao-Chau, which the Kaiser had himself selected—and wisely, it must be admitted—had fallen to an enemy, Japan, whom Germany had least of all expected to engage. This was a bitter blow. Hohenzollern ambitions had never taken such roots in the colonies possessed as in those splendid dream-colonies which others held. Kiao-Chau was a sort of window through which the Hohenzollern—nose pressed close to the glass—might gaze and dream about the empire that was not yet. An attempt had been made to impress China some time before by the brutality of the German soldiery. But the loss of Kiao-Chau undid all this work, and the fact that it had to be surrendered to Japan added a further bitterness. The dream-empire tottered at the first puff of wind.

German South-West Africa Camel Corps. (*Wire Service*)

4

Botha's Campaign in German South-West Africa

T HE TERRITORY KNOWN AS German South-West Africa — an area
equal to that of the German Empire and the United Kingdom
put together, lying between the Orange River and the Portuguese
colony of Angola — passed to German control in 1884, after Great
Britain had refused to give a definite assurance of protection to Herr
Luderitz, who proposed to establish a commercial settlement in
South Africa. It is a wide inhospitable country which before the war
only supported a European population of 14,816, the bulk of whom
were Germans. The chief industry was pastoral; but there are valu-
able copper mines at Otavi, and diamonds to the value of nearly a
million sterling were produced in 1912. Nevertheless, two years
later the expenditure of the colony exceeded the revenue by about
£800,000.

The colony had vast potentialities; but, although much money
had been spent upon its development, it seems to have been regarded before the beginning of the war more as a step towards further
conquest than as a country which might yield much in itself. Its rail-

way system threw out tentacles suggestively near the neighbouring British colonies, and the stores of weapons and ammunition found in it were out of all proportion to the military force. At Tsumeb alone rifles and ammunition were found sufficient, in the judgment of an eyewitness, to equip a force of 20,000 men; and this was the place where the Germans made their last stand. It was the almost invariable fortune of the Imperial troops to find great stores of war material in the towns they occupied.

It is not necessary to look far for the explanation of the accumulation of munitions. The colony was the arsenal for supplying that rebellion of British subjects from the Cape Province for which the German authorities so sincerely wished. The actual rebellion was sufficiently in hand by the end of 1914 for General Botha to undertake in earnest the campaign in German South-West Africa which had been interrupted to cope with it. Maritz* never had any considerable following in his treachery, and hence the German stores of arms were never required.

The invasion of so great a territory was a task which might well have daunted anyone. But General Botha is a soldier of dominating personality with a wide experience in the only sort of campaign by which it could be reduced. His plan was a mixture of caution and daring that is almost unique in history. The conformation of the country dictated its general outlines.

The fertile heart of the country, on which the capital and chief settlements lay, was a tableland, forming a sort of island in the sandy desert country. Across the plateau ran the main railway; and connecting it to civilisation were two great branches to the west, resting upon the only good harbours, Luderitz Bay and Swakopmund.

*Manie Maritz, a Union of South African officer and former Boer general who rebelled against his government and allied himself with the Germans.

Windhoek, the capital of the colony and the site of a great wireless station which could transmit direct to Berlin,* lay nearer the northern branch of the railway, and Botha decided to make that his main line of advance. Another column was to move up the railway from Luderitz Bay, and two other columns were to sweep the southeastern part of the colony towards the main area of the German settlements. The three southern columns were to operate on converging lines, and were eventually to form one southern force under the direction of General Smuts. Pitched battles against fortified positions formed no part of Botha's plan. His was the subtler and more forceful method of sending flying columns towards the rear of such positions, so that the defenders had to choose between retreat and capture.

The Germans thought that Boer General Louis Botha might fight against Britain as he had during the Boer War, but instead Botha led the fight to conquer German South-West Africa. (*Wire Service*)

Yet even the best of plans could not make the conquest of the colony easy. The imperative need of water formed an obstacle which only a bold and ingenious mind could overcome. Almost everything had to be brought from the Cape Province. The wells were found to be poisoned, and although the German commander maintained that this was legitimate warfare, since notices were

*This fact seems to be established. The installation consisted of five steel lattice pillars, nearly 400 feet high, with cable supports.

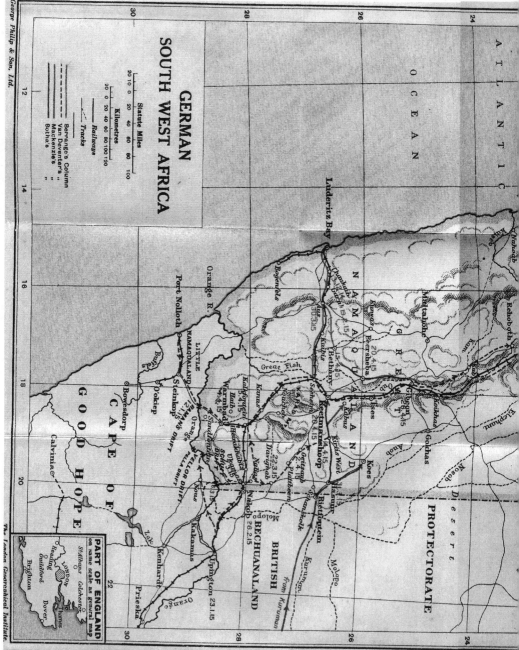

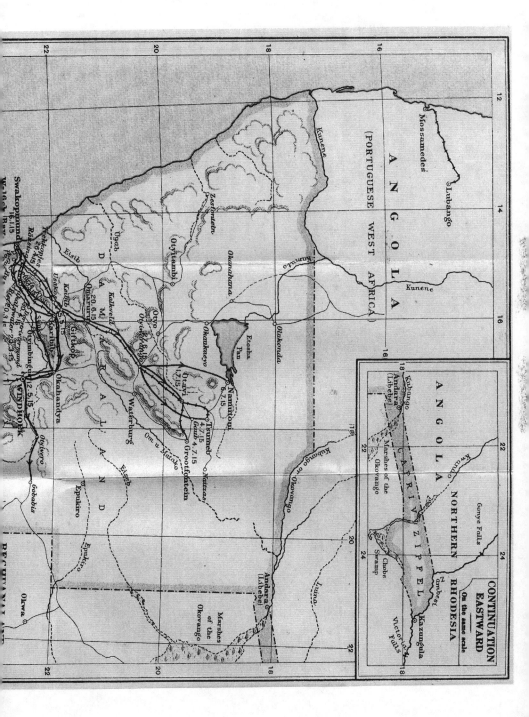

clearly placed at the waterholes, the condition was more honoured in the breach than in the observance. Dense masses of intractable bush, too, formed a barrier that could only be passed at the cost of clothes torn from the back and wounds which refused to heal in the scorching sun. Terrible sand-storms raged almost continuously. Tents were torn to shreds. Railway tracks disappeared in a day, and horses sank to their girths in the soft heaps. The sand invaded the food, and the men could not eat or breathe without consuming it. It caused distressing diseases of the salivary glands, necessitating painful operations and making life burdensome to the soldiers. In some places flies swarmed in such numbers as to cover completely the whole inside surface of the tents.

At the beginning of the year 1915 the two main columns were already in position for their advance. Colonel Beves had reached Luderitz Bay (Luderitzbucht) on September 18th with a force of some 2,000 men,* and when the rebellion broke out. Sir Duncan Mackenzie, with another force destined for Swakopmund, was ordered to divert his course and join Colonel Beves. Luderitz Bay surrendered on September 19th, and there, on what a soldier described as "the worst stretch of country I've ever struck," the troops lay until the time should come for an advance. There were no streams, springs, nor vegetation. The heat was almost unendurable, and the sand-storms beat upon the men like a rain of hot hail. One of the ships conveying the first troops brought fresh water, but further supplies had to be condensed from the sea. Colonel Skinner, with another force of infantry and mounted troops, occupied Walfish Bay, without opposition, on Christmas Day. Mackenzie by this time had established his force at Chaukaib, some 40 miles from the coast.

*Two regiments of infantry, two batteries of artillery, and a squadron of Imperial Light Horse.

The fort at Swakopmund, the most important coastal settlement in German South-West Africa. Swakopmund was established by German colonists in 1892. (*Deutsche Kolonialgesellschaff Bibliothek*)

Meanwhile the British had suffered a complete defeat at Sandfontein. Brigadier-General Lukin had landed at Port Nolloth the sea terminus of the northern railway line in the Cape Province; and, establishing himself at Steinkop, the nearest point to German territory, sent forward a small force to seize the Orange River crossing at Raman's Drift. This was easily accomplished; and a patrol was sent against Sandfontein. The enemy seemed to have left the district; but on September 25th the patrol was attacked, and Colonel Grant, who went to the rescue with reinforcements, was compelled to surrender by a much superior German force on the following day. The invaders had been over-confident; but they also had been the victims of treachery, since Maritz was to have led another British column across the frontier from Upington. If this part of the plans had not miscarried the Germans would not have won their victory.

Even when the rebellion had been broken, Maritz remained at large to give further trouble. On December 22nd he and Kemp attacked a British force near Schuit Drift; but they were driven off by a force of not half the number. About 1,200 strong, they invaded Union territory a month later, and fell upon Upington. Colonel Jacob Van Deventer was then in charge, and on January 24th he drove the rebels off with such energy that within a short time, realising the hopelessness of their position, all of them came in and surrendered.

A German attack on Kakamas, designed to assist Maritz, was also roughly handled, and the Union territory was thenceforward free from further invasion. Maritz disappeared. Part traitor and part dupe, his only justification in German eyes was success. He shared the fate of all traitors in falling under suspicion from his new masters, and found it best to make his escape into Angola.

VAN DEVENTER'S ADVANCE

Colonel Van Deventer speedily gave proof of his generalship. He had to clear a stretch of country of about the same size as Wales, and his method was simple and masterly. One wing was directed to seize and advance by Raman's Drift. The other was to cross the eastern frontier and march via Nakob. The centre was sent across Schuit Drift, with an offshoot crossing the river by Vellor Drift. Before he had met Maritz at Upington, the left wing had already seized Raman's Drift. Colonel Bouwer led this force, and he had secure hold of the river-crossing ten days before Maritz and Kemp made their abortive attack on Upington. Van Deventer's left wing rushed Nakob on February 26th, and, with his flanks both in motion, he marched with his main body towards Schuit Drift. Within a week all the river-crossings were in his hands. A few days later Nabas had been stormed. The enemy held a strongly fortified position; but after five hours' fighting he abandoned it and drew off to Ukamas. It was at this point that Van Deventer, realising the strength of the positions on his main line of advance, determined to make them untenable by a bold turning movement.

Colonel Berrangé was moving across the desert towards Rietfontein with some 2,000 troops. His role was to cut off the force in the southern part of the colony or to compel them to evacuate their positions by the threat to their line of retreat. In this way he was to assist Van Deventer's column, which, concentrating at Kalkfontein, was to move up the railway towards Seeheim. On the eastern flank of the railway were the tangled groups of the Karas Mountains cleft by a defile at

Colonel, later General, Jacob Van Deventer (1874–1922), center, fought in the Boer War and returned to service during World War I leading the Union Defence Forces of South Africa in the German South-West Africa campaign and then the South African Overseas Expeditionary Force mounted brigade in the campaign in German East Africa. (*Library of Congress*)

Noacheb in which a handful of troops could make themselves almost impregnable to frontal attack. Berrangé's force at a certain point must turn this position and cut off the line of retreat of any troops standing there.

But the problem for Van Deventer was whether Berrangé would arrive in time to clear the southern column's advance and whether he would be strong enough to cope with the Germans from the south. To clinch this situation Van Deventer sent his brother, Dirk, with a mobile force to work round the mountains and join Berrangé's western column. Berrangé was timed to cross the frontier about the end of the month. Dirk Van Deventer marched north with the 4th Mounted Brigade, and occupied Davignab, a German police station, on March 22nd. A few days later he found a small force of the enemy entrenched at Plattbeen, and stormed the position. On April 2nd the enemy gave battle at Geitsaub, but was compelled to retire, leaving 16 men prisoners.

Meanwhile, Berrangé was moving towards him with flying patrols, clearing his flank as far north as Koes. The supply of this column was the greatest problem of the campaign. From Kimberley to Rietfontein is about 400 miles. Up to Kuruman (140 miles) asses and oxen formed his transport column, and oxen alone had to supply the remainder of the. distance; but this means of provisionment had to be supplemented by a fleet of fast motor cars. At one part in the line of march 110 miles separated the water-holes, and the strain on the motor transport was therefore extremely heavy. That the 2,000 men* were able to march rapidly ahead in spite of the difficulties of this waste country is a sufficient tribute to the success of the transport.

As Van Deventer crossed Schuit Drift on March 6th, Colonel Berrangé was leaving Kuruman. On the 19th he put to flight an enemy patrol at Schanskolk, and entered Hasuur across the frontier on the last day of the month. A fortnight later Dirk Van Deventer and Berrangé met at Kiriis West, where a patrol sent across country to attack the railway north of Keetmanshoop rejoined him, after driving off the enemy in a violent engagement. But by this time almost the whole south-eastern part of the colony had been cleared.

---

*5th South African Mounted Rifles, the Bechuanaland Rifles, Cullinan's Horse, and the Kalaharia Horse.

Van Deventer had waited until Colonel Bouwer, with the left flank, was beginning his approach to Warmbad before pressing forward to Kalkfontein, which he entered on April 5th, the day after Bouwer had occupied Warmbad. Two days later the whole of the southern column was concentrated at Kalkfontein, and on the 11th General Smuts reached the spot and took over command.

Mackenzie's force, in the meantime, had spent a weary time waiting for the signal to advance. Chaukaib was open to him, in November; but he did not move his camp there until December 13th, and in this desolate place, in a plain particularly defenceless against the sand-storms, the men's only excitement, was the visit of a few German aeroplanes. Patrols who moved out on reconnaissance duty were the envy of the troops. But their lot was not easy. The lack of water is a hardship which nothing can minimise, and it is worthy of the men that man and horse

An Askari soldier in German service. The Ashanti had fought the British throughout the nineteenth century and most allied themselves with Germany during World War I. (*Deutsche Kolonialgesellschaff Bibliothek*)

shared what little was available. Frequently the men poured the last of their water into their helmets that the horses might drink.

Wells and water-holes might be poisoned. Even to approach them might be dangerous. At the beginning of the campaign several men met their death from the land mines sown round the surface of the water-holes. Even the dry river beds were treated in the same way, so that a natural path might not be used by the Union troops.

On February 8th General Botha visited the camp on his way to Swakopmund, and reviewed the troops. There were present the Transvaal Scots in kilts, a large number of Boers, and adventurers,* from all corners of the world; and Botha's reception as he came along the repaired railway in an open truck lacked nothing in enthusiasm. He addressed the men in kindly words, assuring them of the gratitude of the Empire for their services and wishing them God-speed in the coming advance. On February 19th the troops moved out to Garub; but only to be compelled to another long delay there.

At Garub the outposts consolidated their position and waited again. The latest delay had the added sting that it came as a disappointment. Botha's words had suggested the chance of fighting in the near future. But no attempt was made to engage the Germans, who were observed by patrols fortifying the gap in the hills in which Aus lies. Botha again visited the camp on March 26th. Two days later Mackenzie moved his headquarters there, and on the 30th Aus was occupied. There was no resistance. An advance patrol had a narrow escape from a land mine, which blew four mules to fragments; but the enemy abruptly abandoned his positions on the approach of the British. At Aus, Mackenzie hastily concentrated his mounted troops, with adequate supplies, for the dash across the country, which was to give them the only battle in the southern part of the colony. And thus, when General Smuts took over command at Kalkfontein, the three columns in the south were closing in upon Keetmanshoop in a wide arc, and Mackenzie and Berrangé were prepared to close the open sector and cut off the Germans.

---

*The whole of this amazing campaign was carried out by the volunteer forces of the Union. The Burgher troops made an incomparable mounted infantry. For the rest, the force included any who had drifted to South Africa either as a permanent or temporary settlement and had felt the call of the fight for civilisation.

Transvaal Scots soldiers at an assembly point in German South-West Africa. (*Illustrated War News*)

THE MAIN COLUMN BY THIS TIME had moved forward from Swakopmund and had fought one heavy engagement. Colonel Skinner had used his time well at Walfish Bay. He had first to consolidate his position in the former British settlement and then to construct huge condensers to produce the water so imperiously needed. He then concentrated the supplies for the advance into the interior. On January 13th he reconnoitred the coast road to Swakopmund. The expedition was not without incident. At one point, near the beach, a mine exploded under two troopers of the advance guard, blowing them and their horses to pieces.

Three other explosions followed; but these were not the contact mines with which the troops had become familiar. They were fired from the beach, where a German lay in hiding in a packing case covered with sand, the only opening being concealed by seaweed. A telephone connected him with one of the German outposts. The operator remained concealed during the day—his existence unsuspected—and decamped in the darkness, leaving some bedding, books, and a candle behind.

Colonel Skinner found Swakopmund deserted, and promptly decided to occupy it. The wells had been poisoned and the railway mined; but the troops, now led to expect such things, became expert in dealing with them. The engineers attained an extraordinary proficiency in detecting the site of mines and rendering them innocuous, and all wells were pumped out as soon as possible. The final occupation was proclaimed on January 16th, and for three weeks the time was devoted to concentrating supplies. Skinner had an odd fate during this campaign. On two occasions he decided to move against the enemy, only to meet him half-way on the way to attack the Union troops. Just before dawn on February 7th a reconnoitring force moved out and came into contact with a body of the enemy. But the latter retreated after each side had suffered a few casualties.

Four days later General Botha took over the command. After Botha came increasing numbers of Burgher troops, and they were assured of water for their advance by the fact that the Swakop River had been recently in flood—a rare occurrence—which damaged the railway laid in the river bed. But before the advance could be undertaken larger supplies of all sorts had to be concentrated, horses had to be rested after their sea journey, and the Burghers had to become inured to the new conditions. On February 22nd, however, a move eastward and south-eastward was made. The enemy had retired from Nonidas, and was supposed to be at Goanikamtes. Flanking patrols were sent out, and Botha moved directly against the position; but the enemy exploded the ammunition he could not take with him, and fell back once more. Goanikamtes and Husab, each with good wells, were occupied, and the patrols pushed some distance up the Swakop.

Some three weeks later Botha moved out once more. The same enveloping tactics were employed. The enemy was lying at Riet and Pforte, and columns moved against these two places and also against Jakalswater. At Riet the enemy fled after the bombardment, not waiting for the infantry attack; and at Pforte the mounted Burghers rode the defence down. At Jakalswater the column of the Union troops attacked with great vigour and skill, but were unable to force the position; but this, with Riet and Pforte, was abandoned after the engagement. Another pause had then to be made. The transport difficulty was still critical, and while it was being dealt with the southern force was making rapid strides forward.

The Battle of Gibeon

By mid-April, as we have seen, the southern columns were converging in a wide arc upon Keetmanshoop and the main railway. It was at this point that Mackenzie made a dash across country with his mounted troops to attempt to cut the line behind the enemy. Botha had paid another visit to Mackenzie's headquarters, and by April 15th the mounted force had reached Bethany. Five days later he was at Beersheba, where he was held up for a few days to allow his supply column to approach. Keetmanshoop was occupied on this day, and in the evening of the 24th the mounted force rode hard upon Gibeon. A section was sent forward to cut off the retreat north of Gibeon; but it was not strong enough for its task, and in the evening of the 25th it fought a gallant engagement and suffered heavy loss. The following day Mackenzie attacked the German rearguard from three sides, and a vigorous battle developed. It was evenly contested, and although the Union troops could not prevent the enemy's escape, they inflicted heavy loss on him, and virtually ended the southern campaign. The enemy lost 8 killed, 30 wounded, and 166 prisoners, and left behind guns and ammunition.

The converging columns had done their work. Gibeon was the only pitched battle; but the enemy had been compelled by the swift and correlated movements to evacuate all the southern part of the colony, and on April 27th Smuts from Aus proclaimed his occupation of the area. Two days later he was riding across country towards Botha.

THE SURRENDER OF WINDHOEK

Meanwhile, Skinner had again met the enemy as he was approaching to attack. On the night of April 25th he moved out, with a squadron of Imperial Light Horse, from Trekkopjes to reconnoitre the northern railway, and fell back on that place on meeting a large force of the enemy. The following day the Germans attacked for four hours with guns, but then withdrew after suffering loss. Skinner had no artillery; but his infantry* held the position steadfastly, and a British naval armoured car detachment performed excellent service.

It was on this day Botha moved out from Husab and Riet with his mounted troops. Brigadier-Generals Brits, Myburgh, and Manie Botha, with their brigades, moved astride the Swakop River in a widely flung line, Botha travelling by motor car up the centre with a small bodyguard. On the last day of April he had reached Dorstriviermund, and sent Myburgh and Manie Botha to cut off Karibib from the east. Then on May 5th he left the river bed and rode upon Karibib, which he entered without opposition.

The railway was hastening forward at high speed, and with it came the infantry and the necessary supplies of food. The Burgher mounted troops had gone eastward towards Windhoek, the capital, and on May 10th Botha heard that the enemy was ready to surrender the town. He therefore rode across country to receive the surren-

*The 2nd Transvaal Scottish, 2nd Kimberley, and 1st Rhodesian regiments.

South African troops occupying the fort at Windhoek. The fort was built in 1890 at the site of an original African settlement that was further expanded by Afrikaners beginning in the mid-nineteenth century. Following the creation of the German South-West Africa protectorate in 1885, Windhoek became the capital of the colony in 1892. (*Deutsche Kolonialgesellschaff Bibliothek*)

der. Three days were spent on the journey through the bush, and on the 12th the town was formally taken over. The Burgher brigades were waiting outside, and they entered with Botha, who hoisted the flag and addressed his weary troops. Colonel Mentz was appointed Governor of the capital, whose huge wireless station was no longer available to Germany.

The bulk of the enemy had retired to the north; but a small force remained east of Windhoek, and Botha sent a flying column to deal with it. The Union troops were quite successful, and put the enemy to flight, with the capture of 150 prisoners, suffering only one casualty themselves. The Germans now attempted to make terms with Botha, and an armistice for two days was arranged from May 20th. Botha returned to Karibib, and met the German Governor Seitz and Colonel Franke, the military commander, at Giftkop. The terms proposed by the Germans were an armistice until the end of the war, each side retaining the territory then in occupation. Botha, with a complete victory almost in sight, would not agree.

The final operation had now to be prepared. The force which was at Windhoek needed time to rest and refit. The long distance traversed at great speed by infantry as well as mounted troops, with scanty supplies and little water, exacted due toll for the men and horses. The main force which had marched upon Windhoek had marched straight across country from Swakopmund. Travelling in the cooler parts of the day on little sleep, and on quarter and, finally, one-eighth rations, they at length sank into a mood in which incredible marches were performed almost automatically.

In this marvellous trek the men covered 180 miles in five days, and their travel-stained and ragged uniforms were the outward symbol of their utter weariness. Some of the men's hands were masses of raw flesh. The flesh diet without salt or vegetables had produced a condition in which scratches spread into open sores. Marching through the bush had torn their clothes to rags and their skin into wounds. Botha had outstripped his transport column; but even Windhoek, cut off by the Union troops, had for some time been on rations.

THE FINAL ROUND-UP

On June 18th Botha moved out from Karibib for the final round-up of the enemy, who had fallen back to the north-eastern corner of the colony. Adopting the usual crescent form of advance, he went forward rapidly, sweeping the northern railway with his wide arc of troops. Brits, with one column, was out on the left; Myburgh was with another on the right; and Botha moved with two mounted brigades and one of infantry in the centre.

He rapidly passed through Omaruru and Kalkveld, the enemy falling back before the advance, and arrived at Otyiwarango, having

Mounted German South-West Africa troops at Windhoek earlier in the campaign. (*Wire Service*)

travelled over 100 miles in less than a week. He left on June 27th, and on July 1st the troops marched into Otavi. There had been a brief resistance on the previous day, and the approaches to the town had been mined. But the Union force was not to be checked. Three days later the infantry, under General Beves, marched into Otavi, having covered the last 45 miles on quarter rations in 36 hours — probably the most remarkable marching feat in the world's history.

There was an armistice at Otavi; but meanwhile the flanking columns were developing their disposition. Myburgh crossed the railway from Otavi to Grootfontein, and on July 4th routed a small body of the enemy at Gaub, and rode in upon Tsumeb, where the main force lay. He was met by a flag of truce, and was informed that the armistice at Otavi extended to Tsumeb; but he insisted upon communicating with Botha, and, learning that the armistice was only local, he demanded and secured the complete surrender of the town.

Brits on July 6th had appeared at Namutoni, having made a wide detour to cut off the enemy's chance of escape to Angola. He received there the surrender of another troop of the enemy, with their supplies and considerable quantities of munitions. Botha's main force remained at Otavi, and on July 8, 1915, he received the final surrender of the enemy. The German commander had been completely beaten by the astounding speed with which the Union forces marched. Indeed, at the last moment he seems to have refused to believe that the Union dispositions were as we know them to have been. He could not understand how any troops could march such distances in so short a time. His main force lay entrenched across the line from Otavi to Tsumeb, and while he stood in front of Botha's main force on this position Myburgh had entered Tsumeb, and Brits, having taken Namutoni, was moving round to the east.

The Germans surrendered. They had been beaten as much by the superb endurance of the Union troops as by the skill of their leader. If we imagine the Boers in the place of the German commander we realise the lack of initiative he showed. Frequently the Union troops took risks, and an enterprising enemy would have met the columns in detail. Botha himself, on the march to Karibib, had but a small escort, and such a risky venture would have fared badly against Boer troops.

Botha showed himself as prudent in victory as he had been skilful and bold in encompassing it. The enemy troops were to be interned, retaining rifles, but without ammunition. Some 3,500 officers and men, with 37 field guns and 22 machine-guns, surrendered. Officers were to retain arms, and on giving their parole could choose their place of residence. Civil officials were merely asked to give their parole.

From first to last there were about 50,000 troops engaged, and the total casualties amounted to 1,189. The deaths from all causes only amounted to 140. More fell victim to disease than were killed in action, and many died through accident.

The campaign was a triumph of organisation. Guns, horses, medical stores, mules, provisions, much of the water, all the forage, and railway material for repairing the lines, with about 30,000 men, had been brought from the Cape Province some 500 to 700 miles by sea to two ports with no equipment for disembarking. The Burgher troops, who traversed such distances with scanty rations, deserved the praise of their commander. In his general order, Botha said: "The Commander-in-Chief finds in the magnificent work which has been performed so uncomplainingly and resolutely an indication of what may be expected of the citizens, of the Union, who place their duty before personal feelings and interests."

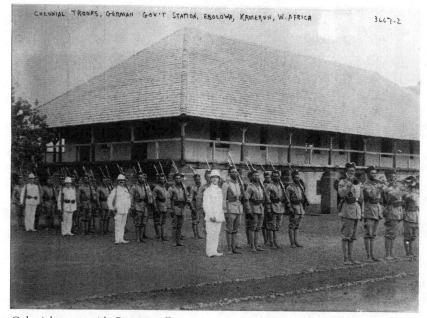

Colonial troops with German officers at a goverment station at Ebolowa, Kamerun. (*Library of Congress*)

5

GERMAN KAMERUN

THOUGH THE GERMANS SHOWED LITTLE more enterprise in the Kamerun campaign than in German South-West Africa, they succeeded in dragging it out for eighteen months, and then carried off the bulk of their forces into the Spanish colony of Rio Muni to the south. The division of command between generals of two nationalities directing operations from headquarters 500 miles apart, with no means of direct communication and the employment of regular troops belonging to three European nationalities, offered the Germans considerable chances. They did not make the most of them; but they could not help profiting by them to some extent, and the escape into neutral territory was directly due to them.

The colony of Kamerun is about 40 percent larger than Germany in Europe, and, in its long span from north to south—from Lake Chad to the Congo—it includes several types of country, though almost everywhere the climate is unhealthy. The coastline is fringed with a border of mangrove swamp, which merges inland into dense forest country. Alligators wallow in the swamps, ever ready for the unwary, and in the forests the natural difficulties of proceeding with a long line of carriers were added to by the gorillas, baboons, and elephants. In one engagement both sides were put to flight by a frenzied elephant, and in another wild bees succeeded in accomplishing what the Germans were unable to do. So dense was the bush between the coast and Yaunde that when the first advance was made the troops had to hack their way through, and could only make a mile a day.

The heart of Kamerun is high and broken country, with coarse, long grasses; the south is generally wetter, lower, and more wooded towards the west; while the north, apart from its mountainous western rim, is more open. The bulk of Kamerun was ceded to Germany by King Bell of Duala in 1884, but the Duala were so harshly treated that they were ready to help the British when General Dobell began operations. About 100,000 square miles was added from French territory in the south and east in 1911 after the Agadir incident.*

It was in this area the first movements of the campaign took place. The Germans had pushed out their territory until it touched the great waterway of the Congo in the south and the only less considerable Ubangi in the east. The French colonists had not forgiven or forgotten these incidents of the Agadir settlement, and in the first week of the war the troops on the spot commenced the redemption of the ceded territory. One column marched down the river and seized Zinga just over the frontier; 5 and another, moving up from the south, occupied Bonga. These two columns pointed like spear-

---

*In July 1911, Germany sent the gunboat *Panther* to the Moroccan port city of Agadir in response to France's deployment of troops to quell a Moroccan independence movement. Both Britain and France viewed Germany's actions as an attempt to establish German presence on the Atlantic. Ultimately, France ceded territory that became part of German Kamerun in exchange for recognizing French authority in Morroco.

heads to the heart of the colony, and the German troops were directed to deal with them.

The German force at the outbreak of the war amounted to 3,500, of which one-third was armed police, and not more than 250 Germans; but by summoning all Germans of military age in the colony to the Colours the number of Germans was increased to 3,000, and at least 20,000 natives were enrolled. They were all well equipped, and their commander, Colonel Karl Zimmermann, proved a cool and skilful leader. The land forces of the Allies never amounted to more than 19,000, of whom 11,000 were French, 600 Belgians, and the rest British. The vast bulk were native troops— splendid soldiers, like the Senegalese or the West African Frontier Force, whose officers boasted that they would go anywhere and do anything and never succumb to depression.

There was but a poorly developed system of communications in the colony, and a further obstacle to its easy conquest was the number of well-selected fortified centres, some of which gave considerable trouble to the invaders.

Before the next acts in the campaign took place the German Foreign Office made an attempt to secure immunity for their colonies in the manner already recorded.

THE NIGERIAN EXPEDITIONS

It was on August 25th that three columns left their bases in Nigeria and moved towards Kamerun. All three met with a check, and two of them suffered serious defeats. One column, under Lieutenant-Colonel G. T. Mair, marching from Ikom on the Cross River, passed over the border and seized Nsanakang; but the small force left there was attacked on September 6th by a large body of enemy troops, and was almost annihilated. Nearly 100 were killed, and when the day was clearly lost two British officers and 90 native soldiers charged the enemy, hacked their way through, and escaped into the bush. After days of terrible hardship, this small body drifted back in twos and threes to British territory. Another column, under Lieutenant-Colonel P. Maclear, marched upon Garua from Yola, and in the night of August 30th captured one of the forts which supported the position. But on the following morning the enemy threw his whole force on the British, and compelled them to fall back from their starting-point.

The third attempt to invade the colony from Nigeria marched upon Mora from Maidugari, and though it failed to reduce this little fortress, it did not fail as disastrously as the other columns. Mora was, like Garua, one of the positions which the Germans had made almost impregnable. It stood on a steep eminence, difficult to approach, and easy to hold. Though Captain Fox's column failed to take it, his force was still investing it when Colonel Brisset, marching from Kusseri, arrived there in mid-October. Kusseri fell to the second assault, for General Largeau had failed to capture the position in the first week of the war.

Thus at the end of the first month of the war all the Allied attempts to invade the colony from the south and north-east frontiers had been checked. Only at one point were the Allies on German territory, and two British columns had suffered summary treatment. In the south-east and east, however, French columns were advancing; but they were as yet too remote a threat to inconvenience the German commander, who had concentrated the bulk of his forces in the central arid north-west part of the colony.

CAPTURE OF DUALA

While these events had been taking place plans were being concerted for a more formidable invasion of the colony. Towards the end of August there appeared off the coast the British cruiser *Cumberland*,

Senegalese troops in French service training with machine guns at the Duala barracks. Once Duala had been secured, it provided a base for further operation against the Germans in Kamerun. (*Wire Service*)

and she was joined by the small gunboat *Dwarf*, which had been hovering in the vicinity for some time. On September 3rd a detachment was landed at Victoria. The German commander ordered it to leave the next day, but as soon as it was embarked the British ships bombarded the town. The Germans had been at work mining the Kamerun River and constructing a barrier; but the *Dwarf* got to work on it and survived a series of adventures which seem as if they were taken from fiction. An unconventional torpedo was towed almost to the side of the vessel, only to miss it by a few feet. Then a large German vessel tried to ram the gunboat, but was itself wrecked. A little later two small motor-launches tried to get home spar torpedoes, but failed. The tiny warship rode safely through all the perils and survived to play a more stirring role.

Meanwhile, Major-General Sir Charles Dobell had been concentrating his force and was approaching the Kamerun estuary. His army comprised about 4,500, half being the West African Frontier Force under their British officers, and the rest the French

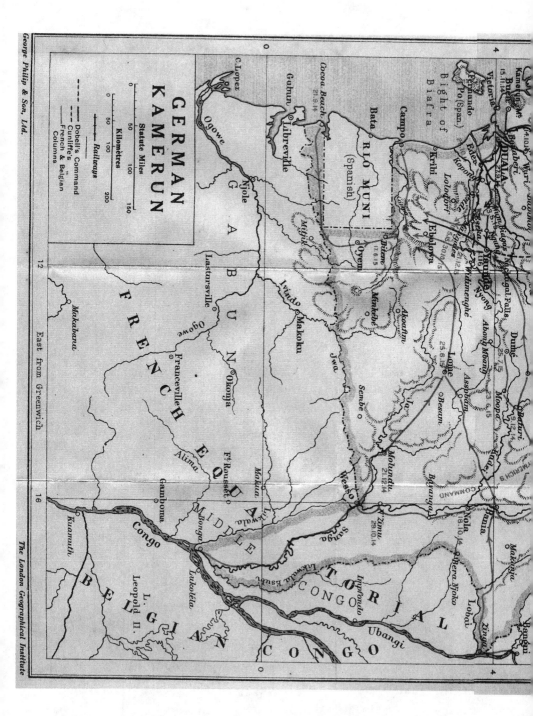

George Philip & Son, Ltd.

GERMAN
KAMERUN

Statute Miles

0   50   100   160

Kilometres

0   50   100   200

- - - - - Dobell's Command
- - - - Cunliffe's
——— French & Belgian
        Columns
——— Railways

East from Greenwich

The London Geographical Institute

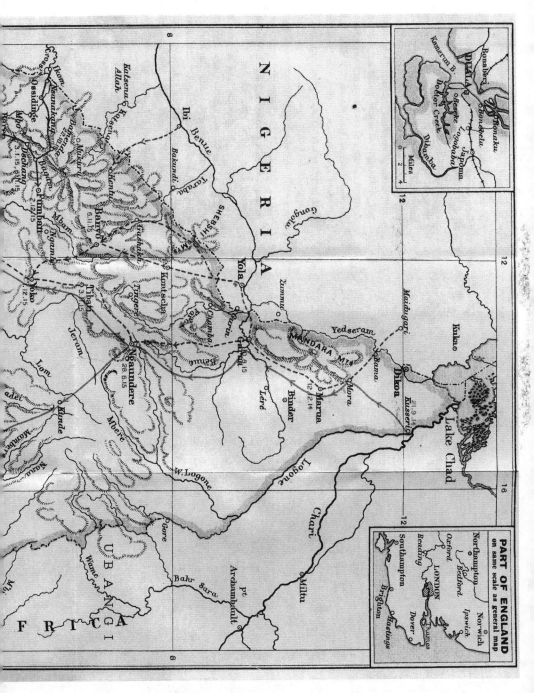

HMS *Challenger* at Duala. The *Challenger* was the lead ship of a class of second class protected cruisers. Laid down in 1900, the warship was completed in 1904. In addition to assisting with the blockade of the German cruiser *Konigsberg*, *Challenger* led the bombardment of Dar-es-Salaam in 1916. (*Wire Service*)

Senegalese tirailleurs under Colonel Mayer. These two bodies of native troops were first-rate soldiers, and if they had been in considerably greater force the campaign could not have dragged on so long.

The troops arrived off the coast in the last week of September, and the light cruiser *Challenger* forced the barrier in the estuary. The shore batteries came into action as the *Challenger* with the *Dwarf* proceeded up the estuary, and destroyed the mines. On September 25th, when the *Challenger* had got Duala, the chief port, under easy range. Sir Charles Dobell summoned the colony to surrender. The Germans refused, and the town was thereupon bombarded. The Governor had left the town, and the Commandant went to Edea as soon as the bombardment opened, leaving Lieutenant Nothnagal in command. During the following day the enemy troops were sent away, and on September 27th the

Senegalese tirailleurs in French service drilling near Duala. The Senegalese were excellent soldiers and highly regarded by both the French and British commanders. (*Wire Service*)

town was surrendered. With it was also surrendered Bonaberi, on the opposite side of the estuary, and eight liners of the Woermann line.

General Dobell did not allow the grass to grow under his feet. Duala and Bonaberi were of capital importance for offensive operations. Duala was the starting-place of the southern railway into the interior, as Bonaberi was of the northern line; and as the rest of the coast was commanded from the sea and the other chief ports occupied, the enemy was cut off from all external help. The Allied grip on Duala and the immediate hinterland was at once consolidated, and preparations were made to clear the railways. The enemy had retreated due eastward to Edea, and General Dobell was first concerned to follow him up. In their retreat the Germans had torn up railways and wrecked the Japoma Bridge over the Dibamba Creek, and they lay entrenched on the farther side of the creek to resist all attempts at crossing. Colonel Mayor's tirailleurs, with the help of the Navy, gallantly broke down this resistance.

In all the earlier operations from the coast the Navy did its share. For days the men would be sent up stream in armed pinnaces, fighting from the water or landing parties to turn positions. All sorts of river-craft were forced into service. Armed with 12-pounders, these could co-operate in the coast reaches of the rivers. In this amphibian life the naval men showed their usual versatility and capacity for endurance. Even on rations reduced to a half or a quarter the normal allowance, they were capable of working round the clock.

Colonel Zimmermann had retreated to Edea, whither the Governor had also withdrawn. Edea lies on the southern railway; but it also stands on the banks of the Sanaga, the largest of the Kamerun rivers which empty themselves into the Atlantic. An armed flotilla sailed for Edea under the command of Commander L. W. Braithwaite, while two columns marched upon it by land. The chief difficulty in their advance was the problem of transport. Almost everything had to be carried by natives, each with his load of 50 pounds on his head, and as the advance was strongly resisted, it required no small inducement to infuse courage into the great number of bearers. But in face of the converging columns from land and sea, the Germans fell back upon Yaunde, 100 miles east of Edea, and this town was occupied on October 26th.

Meanwhile, General Dobell was dealing with the enemy north of Duala. Land and river forces were sent against Jabassi. The flotilla sailed up the Wuri River, and was lying off the town at the end of the first week of October. But the place was strongly held, and the native soldiers proved unequal to their first encounter with machine-guns. The attack was beaten off. A second attempt was made on October 14th with the help of naval rivercraft, and Jabassi fell into British hands.

At the same time other columns were spreading out fanwise from Duala. Buea, the summer resort, lying at the foot of Kamerun Mountain, was the objective of two columns under Colonel Gorges and Lieutenant-Colonel Rose, who marched upon the town, while a demonstration was made by the Navy against Victoria. The town was occupied in the middle of November, and Colonel Gorges' force went to reinforce a column under Lieutenant-Colonel H. H. Haywood, which was clearing the northern railway. Nkongsamba, the terminus, was captured on December 10th, and with it two aeroplanes, not yet unpacked. Colonel Gorges marched swiftly north, and three weeks later had destroyed the fort at Dschang. He then fell back to Bare, where Colonel Rose had established an outpost from Nkongsamba.

German Attack on Edea

It was while Colonel Gorges was at Dschang that the Germans made their only attempt at serious offensive operations during the campaign. But on this occasion, as so frequently during the campaign, they were forced to pay for their ill-treatment of the native population. Directly a plan was matured, some native (man or woman) would disappear in the bush and carry the news to the Allies. Thus the attack almost invariably lost the advantage of the surprise. Colonel Zimmermann at the end of the year laid his plans for a sudden blow at Colonel Mayor's troops. Edea was to be assaulted simultaneously with its outpost Kopongo, a few miles to the east. But, being forewarned, the little force, with its block-house at Kopongo, was reinforced, and was able to beat off with loss an attack by 150 Germans on January 5th.

Edea was differently situated. It lay in a narrow clearing in the forest which surrounded the straggling settlement, offering every opportunity to an assault. Nevertheless, the town had been carefully forti-

African troops in German service in Kamerun. The troops are equipped with German supplied uniforms and rifles. (*Deutsche Kolonialgesellschaff Bibliothek*)

fied, and the tirailleurs proved such cool and skilful shots that when the attack came it met with a costly defeat. The enemy column was almost 1,000 strong, armed with machine-guns; but after a prolonged engagement it was forced to withdraw, leaving 111 dead. Of these, 23 were Europeans, 6 being officers. There were also 102 native soldiers wounded.

Hence, in the first week of the New Year the Allies had established their hold over a considerable range of country from Nkongsamba to Edea. But General Dobell realised by this time the inadequacy of his force. A country of such dimensions tended to swallow up troops in vast numbers. The enemy's plan was simply to hold where he could until he was driven out, and the risks to long columns marching into the interior were far too great to be undertaken without much ampler resources than were, at the time, at General Dobell's disposal. The Allied Commander accordingly applied for reinforcements.

FRENCH ADVANCE INTO INTERIOR

Considerable headway had been made in the meantime by the columns operating from the east, south-east, and north-east. The forces which had occupied Zinga and Bonga were merely small French detachments; but General Aymerich, who commanded the troops in French Equatorial Africa, quickly reinforced them, put them under able commanders, and sent them ahead. Colonel Morrison commanded the column at Zinga, which rapidly ascended the Lobai, crossed the Upper Sanga, meeting at Bania the Sanga force under Colonel Hutin; and by the end of September had covered 200 miles and occupied Camot. The speed of this advance disconcerted the enemy; and hence, when he pushed westward, Morrison was able to occupy Baturi, and towards the end of December even reached Bertua. A vigorous engagement took place there; but the French occupied the town, though they were conscious that in the retreat the German forces were concentrating. Hence, on pushing forward to Dume, they were met by a superior force and compelled to fall back east of Bertua.

Colonel Hutin's advance was even more rapid at the beginning. With a versatile river force moving with him, he had captured the fortified town of Nola by mid-October. He had thus covered 300 miles from his starting-place; but in so doing he left a long exposed line of communications behind him. The Germans seized their chance, and, marching from Mohmdu, on the Ja—a tributary of the Sanga—they cut Hutin's communication at N'Zimu.

General Aymerich, with a small Belgian river force, marched rapidly north to turn the enemy out. The small Belgian boat, the *Luxemberg*, took more than its share of the three days' fighting. The town was attacked from the land as well as from the river side; and the *Luxemberg*, braving the heavy fire, steamed up to short rifle range of the German positions, and kept up a galling and destruc-

A German supply column making its way to Garua (*Deutsche Kolonialgesellschaff Bibliothek*)

tive fire from its small guns, until at last the enemy broke and fled, leaving many dead behind. From this time — the end of October — until the end of December, Colonel Hutin had to devote himself to clearing the enemy from his flank. Molundu fell on December 21st, and shortly afterwards the French resumed their march towards Lome.

SURRENDER OF GARUA

Colonel Brisset, as we have seen, had captured Kusseri, in the north-eastern corner of Kamerun, in September, and he then marched to Mora, where he found the small British force under Captain Fox. He then made one of the many unsuccessful attempts to storm this position. After his failure he marched south upon Marua, and captured it in mid-December.

There had been more border activity between Nigeria and Kamerun; but it was felt that the effect of the forces available was minimised owing to the lack of unity in the direction, and accord-

Emplacements at Garua. The fort finally surrendered after a heavy bombardment by Allied forces which included a 12-pounder and gun crew taken from the HMS *Challenger*. (*Deutsche Kolonialgesellschaff Bibliothek*)

ingly Brigadier-General F. J. Cunliffe, of the Nigeria Regiment, was put in command of the French and British forces in February. After consultation with General Dobell, he went north. He decided that the northern fortified positions could not be reduced without guns, and he was able to secure a 12-pounder from the *Challenger** and, a little later, a 95mm from the French. His first objective was the reduction of Garua.

The necessity of dealing with this fortress was unpleasantly emphasised by an assault upon the small British frontier post Gurin, early in April. The garrison at Gurin held a small mud fort outside of the town, with 40 native soldiers, a white sergeant, and Lieutenant Pawle. Mr. J. F. Fitzpatrick, a political agent, was also present. The assaulting force comprised 400 native infantry, 40

*The adventures of the naval detachment, which, under Lieutenant L. H. Keppel Hamilton, took this gun 700 miles across Africa, deserves a chapter to themselves. It was first conveyed 160 miles up the Niger, then 480 miles up the Benue, and finally 60 miles across country.

being mounted, and 16 Europeans, with four maxim guns. The attack lasted several hours, and 60,000 rounds were fired by the maxims. Lieutenant Pawle fell almost at the beginning, and the sergeant was wounded. But Mr. Fitzpatrick took command, and the assailants were beaten, with a loss in dead alone almost equal to the whole of the defending force. The following day a relieving force arrived from Yola, after a march of 62 miles in 22 hours. The whole force then marched upon Garua, and Colonel Brisset there joined it.

Hauptmann von Crailsheim, the commander at Garua, was a skilful leader. His attack upon Gurin suggests something of his character, and at Garua he had a position of exceptional strength. The river protected it on the south and, with three outlying forts on the neighbouring hills and one in the plain, he had formed a perfect entrenched camp. In the beginning of the siege he made a daring night sortie with half the garrison, attacked a British post, but without success; then made an uninterrupted march of 28 hours through virgin country, and so, eluding a force sent to intercept him, regained Garua.

From May 28th, when the French 95 mm gun appeared, the two "heavy" pieces kept up an intermittent bombardment. By degrees the assailants had crept up to within 1,000 yards of one of the forts, and on June 9th the enemy, seeing the end approaching, made several attempts to force a way across the river. But the waters were in flood, and the bulk of those who took to it were drowned. The following day the German commander surrendered. The guns had shattered the nerve of the native soldiers, and they refused to fight. A column was at once sent towards Ngaundere under Colonel Webb-Bowen, who, attacking the place in a tornado, put the garrison to flight on June 28th, driving them off towards Tibati.

First March On Yaunde

But by this time one of the saddest misadventures of the campaign had happened. General Dobell had been asked in March to co-operate with the French from the east in an attack upon Yaunde. He agreed, despite his misgivings, and sent a strong column due eastward, north of the railway, under Colonel Haywood. The difficulty was the lack of certainty about effective co-operation between the French, marching from the east, and the columns marching from the west. Colonel Haywood's column marched rapidly eastward, despite strong opposition, and on May 3rd came upon the enemy entrenched on the farther side of the Mbila River at Wum Biagas. The engagement here was so fierce and prolonged that though the British took the position after 18 hours' fighting, they had suffered serious loss.

Colonel Mayer, however, had, under cover of the diversion, followed the railway eastward, and on May 11th occupied the terminus, Eseka. He then went to Wum Biagas to take charge of the main operations. He had with him about 2,000 troops, but all except 300 were already tired from the fatigues of the advance. He had also a naval 12-pounder, some 80mm guns, and a number of machine-guns. But before he set out on May 25th, General Dobell had been informed that the French had not made the expected headway, and could promise no effective support.

The expedition was therefore doomed to almost certain failure before it began the advance. Yet, with their long line of native carriers, the troops went boldly forward. Supplies came with little regularity. The column struck dense bush, and had to hack a way through. Snipers lay in wait for the long straggling line, and the native carriers at times gave way to panic, and, dropping their burdens, bolted. At unexpected points the troops would come upon machine-guns, and the enemy several times cut the communications. Owing to such mischances, the rate of advance sank to a mile a day.

Dysentery broke out, and Colonel Mayer, loath to give in, asked for more men. A number were sent, and also more carriers; but on June 5th it became clear that the project was impossible of attainment, and the force was ordered to retire. The rainy season was in full swing, but a reinforcement, sent to cover the retreat, arrived, after an incredible march, in the nick of time. With a force smaller by a quarter than when he had set out, Colonel Mayer fell back, and by the end of June had arrived at a position he could hold.

It was one of the odd mischances that must befall forces operating at vast distances from each other that, just as Colonel Mayer gave up his hope, the French columns in the east were making headway once more. Colonel Morrison got his column under way again in May, and after an unsuccessful attack at the beginning of the month, Moopa was captured, after bombardment by a 80mm gun on June 23rd. A month later Bertua was re-taken, and on July 25th Dume was entered. In late June Lome had been captured by Colonel Hutin; the French force was thus established in a threatening position with regard to Yaunde, when it was no longer of immediate value.

Capture of Banyo

Heavy rains had set in, and General Dobell could not take his part in the combined movement on Yaunde until September 22nd. After the fall of Ngaundere, General Cunliffe, finding that Generals Dobell and Aymerich were not yet prepared for the final advance, had taken up strong positions at Ngaundere, Kontscha, and Gashaka; and on August 23rd he commenced a personally directed attack upon Mora. The troops fought with the utmost bravery. A foothold was gained on the summit in one desperate encounter, and a detachment of the 1st Nigerian Regiment clung to a position not 60 yards from the enemy trenches for two days without food or water. The hill was defended with such skill that no one could re-supply the men, and General Cunliffe was forced to recall his troops. The attack was abandoned on September 17th, and no further attempts were made against the position.

Generals Aymerich and Dobell were both advancing when General Cunliffe began his offensive in the north. He had about 4,000 men in October when he marched against Tibati, Banyo, and Bamenda. Tibati fell to Colonels Brisset and Webb-Bowen on November 3rd. Bamenda was occupied by Major Crookenden on October 22nd. He was assisted in this operation by the column of Colonel Cotton, which marched from the northern railway; and the two columns met at Bagam.

The capture of Banyo was a more formidable undertaking. The dwelling part of the settlement was captured on October 24th; but the enemy was entrenched on a neighbouring hill that rose steeply from the plain. The attack began on the morning of November 4th. Under cover of fog, one company, under Captain Bowyer Smith, reached the summit; but he was shot, and the men were forced to the foot once more. When darkness fell, five companies were half-way up and holding on as best they might against incessant fire directed by fireballs and rockets. Next day the troops crept ahead, despite the fire and the rolling down of rocks upon them.

The three 3-inch guns had slowed down, and were just giving out when more ammunition arrived, and they could start again. During the night there was a terrible storm; but the men stood to the positions, and the next morning a white flag was seen flying from the summit. Most of the enemy had escaped during the night, but the rest were compelled to surrender. On the top of the hill broken furniture, bottles, and gramophones were littered about among pigs and sheep. Everything showed that the hill was to have been held to the end; and but for the extraordinary courage and persistence of the assailants it would have been.

GENERAL ADVANCE ON YAUNDE

General Cunliffe's column then turned towards Yaunde. Fumban was captured by Colonel Cotton and Major Uniacke on December 3rd, a day after Brisset had entered Yoko. The troops pressed ahead towards Nachtigal Falls, and made contact with the French from the east. On January 8th they were within 40 miles of Yaunde when they heard that the place had already fallen.

The main force under General Dobell had been growing stronger,* and it had made great headway by November, when it was nearly 8,000 strong.

Mayor's force operated separately against the Yaunde-Kribi road. Eseka was reoccupied on October 30th; but the further advance was violently resisted, and Mangales was not captured till December 21st. Meanwhile, the British column advancing north of the French from Wum Biagas had also encountered stubborn resistance; but by the end of November it had captured Ngung, after hacking its way through almost impenetrable bush.

On December 17th the British fought another successful engagement. Mayer was nearing Mangales. But Dobell instructed the British to go ahead without waiting for him, and after the first five days the enemy positions were found to be abandoned. Colonel Gorges, with the British column, entered Yaunde on January 1st without opposition.

*The reinforcements consisted mainly of Indian troops.

Disarming the Mora garrison. The stronghold at Mora held out against Allied pressure for more than a year after all other areas of Kamerun had surrendered. Mora was the last German controlled territory in West Africa. (*Wire Service*)

THE GERMANS HAD RECOGNISED THE meaning of the lines that were converging upon them and had evacuated the town. Colonel Zimmermann, with over 800 Germans and some thousands of native troops and carriers, had left with Herr Ebermaier for Spanish Muni, about 120 miles distant. Columns were sent in pursuit. Colonel Morrison and Colonel Haywood marched towards the Spanish territory. A week after the occupation of Yaunde, Haywood caught a rearguard at Koimaka on the Nyong, and released some prisoners.

The French force which had landed at Campo in 1914 co-operated, but the troops could not prevent the enemy escaping into neutral territory. They were far too weak for the tasks they attempted. They had cleared the strip of country between Spanish Muni and Gabun, and had taken Bitem in June, 1915; but they could not close the whole of the Spanish frontier. On January 18th the enemy had passed Ebolowa, and in the first week in February was over the frontier. The Germans were later interned in Spain.

Hauptmann von Raben, who still held Mora, was given honourable terms, and surrendered. The vast territory was thus left wholly in the hands of the Allies, and with its fall the German flag disappeared from West Africa, and was only to be found, outside Europe, in German East Africa.

The campaign was skilfully executed. It had to cope with almost incredible difficulties in the matter of communications. Generals Cunliffe and Aymerich each had to improvise a system of supply for communications over 400 miles long. Neither had the slightest help from railways. Yet the various columns of British, French, Belgians, West African natives, and Indians moved inexorably forward on a converging scheme that resembled a complicated game of chess.

An African field battery in German service in East Africa. (*Wire Service*)

6

GERMAN EAST AFRICA

T HE LARGEST OF THE GERMAN COLONIES, German East Africa, lay between British East Africa on the north and Portuguese East Africa on the south. Westward it stretched to the great lakes and the Belgian Congo. Its seaboard on the Indian Ocean, about 450 miles in extent, comprised several good harbours, whose value, however, was diminished by the proximity of the islands Zanzibar and Pemba, which are a British protectorate. In area, the colony was almost twice the size of Germany; and from Uganda to Portuguese East Africa was a march of over 1,000 miles. Its frontier was half as long again as all the battle-fronts in Europe put together.

The bulk of the country is a tableland, and the elevated areas comprise some 50,000 square miles—not quite a seventh of the total area—suitable for European habitation. The hill country west of Dar-es-Salaam and the high stretch of Usambara formed the chief settlements, since the flat coastal border below them was extremely fertile. In some places the highlands rise into mighty peaks, like those of Meru (14,950 feet) and Kilimanjaro (19,321 feet), the highest mountain in Africa. Much of the territory, indeed, gave evidences of a more massive moulding than is common in Africa. The west was cut by the great Rift Valley, in which lay those mighty and splendid lakes which so amaze the traveller.

Strangely ironical is the fate that gave to Germany a country with so many associations with British explorers and missionaries. But so it was arranged, Kilimanjaro going to the Germans because it was first sighted by a German, and because—so it is said—the present Kaiser was interested in its "flora and fauna." The colony was little developed until the accession of Demburg to the Colonial Office, and the Central Railway, from Dar-es-Salaam to Lake Tanganyika, was only completed in February 1914. The usual lack of insight characterised the German dealing with the natives. Indeed, Dr. Schnee, the Governor since 1912, was even at the end of 1913 making inquiries among the district commissioners as to whether Islam might not be completely prohibited. An instruction sent round—a copy of which is now in British hands—directed the commissioners to consider whether the cultivation of pig-breeding might not be an effective means of eradicating Mohammedanism. It was only when the war broke out that the German administrators showed a sudden conversion to Islam in order to enroll Arab volunteers, and in deceiving the Mohammedans the Germans achieved considerable success. But the natives on the frontier were removed inland, as it was thought they might join the Allies; and the behaviour of the chiefs in the north-west shows that the German fears were not without foundation.

AT THE OPENING OF THE WAR THE COLONY was surrounded by enemy territory everywhere except on the south. It was not until March 1916, that Portugal joined the Entente Powers; and the campaign may be roughly divided into two phases by that event. Up to that time the commander of the enemy forces. Colonel Von Lettow-Vorbeck, contrived to keep the Allied forces out of his territory. His force at the outbreak of war consisted of 250 Germans and 2,500 natives; but there were in the colony about 3,000 Germans of military age. There were also a number of Army officers and other German visitors who had arrived at Dar-es-Salaam to celebrate the completion of the Central Railway; and the destruction of the *Konigsberg* in the Rufigi River added another 600 Germans. At its maximum

A German poster for colonial war funds featuring General Paul Emil von Lettow-Vorbeck leading African soldiers. (*Library of Congress*)

strength, with Arab volunteers and native reservists, the force may have amounted to between 20,000 and 30,000; but when General Smuts took over the command he estimated it at 16,000, with 2,000 Europeans, 60 guns, and 80 machine-guns.

With so large a force at the enemy's disposal, the conquest of the colony was a serious undertaking; and for over eighteen months no serious attempt was made to cope with it. The skirmishes that occurred were mostly fought on British territory. Von Lettow-Vorbeck divided his force into three parts. The most important operated in the north-east under Major Kraut; a second, under the retired Prussian General Kurt von Wahle, lay in the north-west and

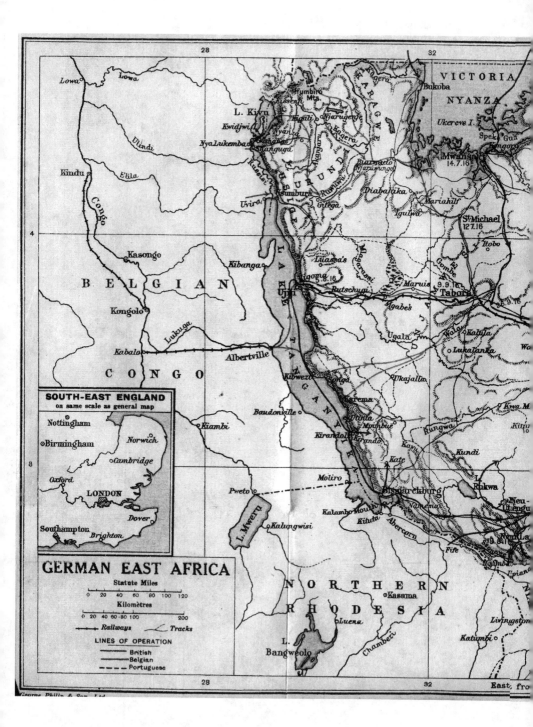

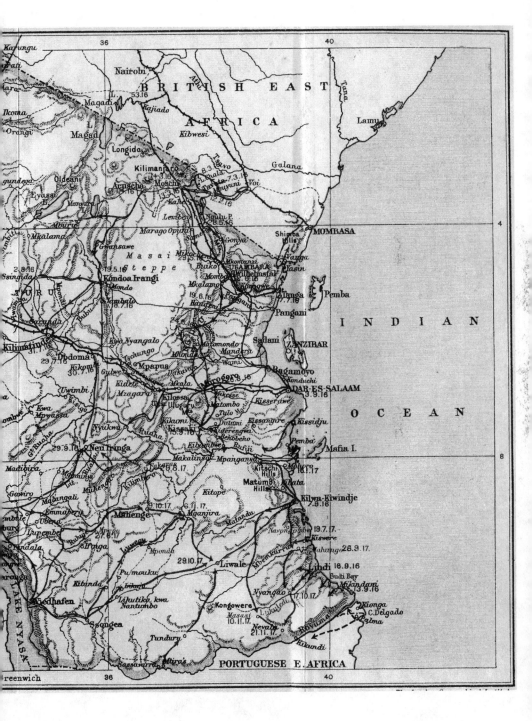

Tabora area; and the third operated against the Nyassa territory under Count Falkenstein. The Allies had no sufficient force at their disposal, though the British settlers at once flocked to the Colours and the Mohammedans were anxious to give every help. The Sultan of Zanzibar, in a letter to his agent at Mombasa, contrasted the British and German methods of dealing with his co-religionists, and summoned them to be faithful to the British.

Hostilities were opened by the British, who sent the cruisers *Astraea* and *Pegasus* on August 8th to bombard Dar-es-Salaam. The German survey vessel *Möwe* and a floating dock were sunk, and a landing party destroyed the wireless station. A week after the bombardment the British settlement at Taveta was captured by a small German force. It was a clever stroke, since Taveta was the chief door into German East Africa from the British colony to the north. At the same time the Germans established a strong outpost on Mount Longido as a northern defence to the Kilimanjaro area. With these operations commenced a series of raids on the railway from Mombasa to Victoria Nyanza (the Uganda Railway), which continued until the end of 1915. The destruction of the railway, which lies nowhere more than 80 miles from the German colony, would have been a serious blow. The raids were boldly conceived, and even contemplated the occupation of Nairobi, the capital of British East Africa, and the capture of the Governor.

Reinforcements were being hurried to British East Africa from India, and with them came Brigadier-General J. M. Stewart to take command. He was at once called upon to meet a determined attack towards Mombasa. The Germans intended to assault simultaneously by land and sea. The *Konigsberg*, one of the fast German cruisers still at large, had suddenly appeared at Zanzibar, and, finding the *Pegasus* practically defenceless, completely disabled her from long range. She also sank the guard-ships *Cupid* and *Khalifa*. The

German government buildings at Dar-es-Salaam buring after the Allied bombardment. The German East African Company established their headquarters at Dar-es-Salaam in 1887. (*Deutsche Kolonialgesellschaff Bibliothek*)

German cruiser was to attack Mombasa from the sea while the land forces assaulted from the west.

The Germans sent raiding parties towards the railway and, marching along the coast, seized Vanga. The advance was made by between 1,000 and 1,500 men, and the expedition, combined with the attack by the *Konigsberg*, looked so serious that women and children were removed from Mombasa, with specie and rolling stock. On the direct route to Mombasa an entrenched camp had been constructed in a mangrove swamp, and a block-house was built. The place was held by Lieutenant Wavell, with 130 Arabs he had raised on the coast. The Germans attacked the camp in force; but were beaten off, though Wavell was severely wounded in the long engagement. Reinforcements reached him from the King's African Rifles and, later, from the Jind Infantry. But in the meantime the *Konigsberg* had been forced to run from British warships, and she only achieved safety by beaching herself up the River Rufiji. On

October 8th a determined attack farther north was beaten off with loss. All the British officers were wounded; but Colour-Sergeant Sumani (a native) assumed command, and headed a charge that routed the enemy. If they could have taken Mombasa the most convenient British port would have been lost; but as a result of the second defeat the enemy was forced back to the frontier.

Several vigorous engagements had been fought about the Tsavo River and near Mount Longido during September; but all were beaten off with the greatest bravery, generally by inferior British forces. It was here that the British first experienced a new horror of war. Some of the wounded were missed, and lay all night in the bush surrounded by wild beasts, while the dead were found to be half-eaten.

THE BATTLE OF TANGA

As so little had come of these incursions, which yet kept the frontier in a state of nervousness, it was decided to attempt to clear the whole region from Kilimanjaro to the coast as far as Tanga. An expeditionary force was to seize Tanga at the same time that the troops assaulted Kilimanjaro. Both operations failed. Tanga, the port of the Usambara highland settlement, was reached by the transports from India on November 2nd. Major-General Aitken had with him about 6,000 troops; but the Germans had got wind of the attack, and Tanga was held in considerable force. The town, reported to be undefended, was summoned to surrender, and refused.

Some hours later a small force was landed south of the town, but it encountered a vigorous resistance in the dense bush, and had to retire and await reinforcements. At 11 A.M. on the 4th the attack was renewed; but again heavy fire was encountered half a mile out of the town. Canes and wires had been cunningly laid in the bush which, when trodden upon, signalled the range to the German gun-

The German light cruiser *Konigsberg* lies scuttled in the Rufiji River. The ship's surviving crew eventually joined General von Lettow-Vorbeck's forces, while its armament, especially its 4.2-inch guns became the heaviest artillery for the Germans in the theater. (*Wire Service*)

ners by moving flags or drew the lids from hives of wild bees. Many of the men suffered terribly from these little pests.* The troops persisted in their attack, and actually entered the town; but the fire from the houses was so fierce that the troops were withdrawn, reembarked, and proceeded to Mombasa. The battle seems to have lacked direction, and the troops who entered the town looked in vain for the support they needed. The total casualties were 795, including 141 British officers and men. The completeness of this reverse discredited the German party, which was in favour of coming to terms with the British, and the soldiers were henceforward unchallenged.

Despite the severity of the reverse at Tanga, part of the troops falling back to the coast were sufficiently unimpressed to strip and bathe. They were found in the water later by the Germans, who

*Later in the campaign the abundance of honey they provided made up for the lack of sugar.

informed the bathers that they were beaten and had better retire! After some parleying, the British agreed to go; but even then they went off in the boats at their leisure. Such spirit deserved a better fate than the defeat of Tanga.

The attack on Longido failed to capture the enemy's position, and the troops were compelled to fall back for water. The main attack was delivered at daybreak on November 4th, and lasted till 7.30 P.M. Later on Longido was found to be evacuated, and was for some time held by the British.

The coastal force in British East Africa fared better. The Vanga Field Force by the end of the year had cleared British territory of the enemy, though an assault towards Taveta made in November had proved as unsuccessful as those made on Tanga and Kilimanjaro. On January 2nd, Yasiri, a port two miles south of the frontier, was captured, and the whole of Umba River valley was seized. The small garrison under Colonel Ragbir Singh repelled a sudden enemy attack ten days later; but on the 18th an assault in force was made, and the garrison held out until their ammunition was used up and their commander dead. The relieving force was not strong enough; but one of the native soldiers brought back his machine-gun with many apologies for having left the tripod! With the recapture of Yasin went also that of Vanga; but little else happened on this frontier for the rest of the year. The raids on the railway were continued at intervals, and the Germans widened and strengthened their holding round Taveta.

Such was the position when, in April, Brigadier-General M. J. Tighe arrived to assume command. Dar-es-Salaam had been again bombarded in December and the shipping destroyed. On this occasion the Navy suffered some casualties from the enemy, who fired on the boats from beneath a white flag. A month later the island of Mafia, at the mouth of the Rufigi, was occupied, and in February a

Indian troops anding at Kissimani Beach, Mafia Island, just off the coast of German East Africa. An English officer is conspicuous in his white uniform and sun helmet at the bow of the boat in the background. Mafi Island served as an observation point for Allied bombardments of German positions. (*Wire Service*)

formal blockade of the coast was instituted, chiefly to prevent gun-running. If this had been completely effective the campaign could not have dragged on so long. But two blockade runners got through, one even in the spring of 1916, and replenished the supplies of ammunition when they were falling low.

THE GERMANS HAD CONDUCTED AN ENERGETIC offensive on their other borders. The Victoria Nyanza has an area equal to that of the whole of Scotland. The Uganda Railway terminates at the lake port Kisumu. Karungu, a British post nearer the German border, was occupied early in September. Like all these frontier posts, it had merely a handful of men as its garrison, and no resistance could be made. When the *Winifred*, a vessel of the Uganda Railway Marine, approached the port a few days later with two squadrons of East African Rifles, it found the Germans in possession, and was compelled to return by the only armed German vessel on the lake, the

Mwanza. A few days later a small British column fought an eight-hours' engagement at a settlement a few miles to the north, and both sides withdrew in the dusk. But it was later discovered that the Germans had even abandoned Karungu. In January the British marched across the border and captured Shirati, and two months later drove off the Germans in disorder midway between the two frontier posts, a few days after the *Mwanza* had been disabled.

In Uganda the natives were asked to hold their Southern frontier, and this they did by seizing the line of the Kagera River south of the frontier. A violent attack was made on them in November; but, in the main, they held their position. This, however, did not protect them from the raids made from time to time across their borders, and General Tighe determined to relieve them by destroying the port Bukoba, which acted as German base, with ample stores and a wireless installation. An advance was to be made from the Kagera, and another column, under General Stewart, was to sail across the lake. In Stewart's command were Colonel Driscoll's detachment of Frontiersmen (later the 25th Fusiliers), including the famous Captain F. C. Selous.* At dawn on June 22nd the troops landed from the lake below Bukoba. The engagement was interrupted almost at its beginning by a tropical downpour of rain; but after that the British made short work of the resistance, and the Lancashires, entering the town from the west, drove the enemy off in disorder. A considerable amount of ammunition and stores was secured, and the troops reembarked the following day, after a complete victory.

LAKE TANGANYIKA WAS DOMINATED ALMOST TO the end of 1915 by the Germans, who had the vessels *Hedwig von Wissmann* and

---

*Not the least romantic incident of an adventurous life was this soldiering at 64 years of age. He was granted the D.S.O. for "conspicuous gallantry"; but he did not survive the campaign.

A German machine-gun boat on Lake Tanganyika. (*Deutsche Kolonialgesellschaff Bibliothek*)

Kingani and, later, the *Kigoma* on the lake. These bombarded the Belgian part of Lukuga (since called Albertville) and other Belgian settlements, and went as they would until two British armed motor-launches* arrived. The *Kingani* was captured and the *Hedwig von Wissmann* sunk very speedily. To the north of Lake Tanganyika, after the customary border struggle, the Belgians secured themselves on the German side of the frontier.

Below Tanganyika lie Rhodesia and the Nyassaland Protectorate — the latter a narrow strip along Lake Nyassa. With the greatest promptitude after the outbreak of the war, the Governor of Nyassaland, Sir George Smith, dispatched the *Gwendolen*, a small steel gunboat, to deal with the only German steamer on the lake —

---

*The adventures of these motor boats, *Mimi* and *Tou-Tou*, which were moved from Cape Town to Tanganyika, more than 2,800 miles overland, are a story in themselves. Special bridges had to be built for the traction engines that drew them up hill and down dale, across desert and through dense bush, to their destination.

Top, the British armed motorboat *Mimi* being readied at Lake Tanganika. Bottom, the *Mimi* and her sister motorboat, *Tou-Tou*, preparing for action on the lake. These boats reached their destination after having been painstakingly moved overland nearly 3,000 miles from South Africa. (*Wire Service*)

British officers, troops, and local persons watch the action of the British motorboats attacking German watercraft on Lake Tanganika. (*Wire Service*)

the *Hermann von Wissmann*. She was discovered in Sphinxhaven,* a small German port, and disabled on August 13th; and the lake was then free from enemy interference. The troops in the Protectorate were few, and though, as usual, volunteers came in readily, it was but a small force that Captain C. W. Barton had at his disposal at Karonga, a northern port 20 miles from the frontier. A German patrol had crossed into British territory, and Captain Barton determined to attack it. By an odd coincidence, the two forces passed each other in the night. At 7 A.M. the next morning (September 9th) a double company of the King's African Rifles was sent ahead to attack a small force of the enemy. Within an hour gunfire was heard at Karonga, where only 10 Europeans and 50 natives had been left, with three women. A double company, under Captain Griffiths, was sent back, and completely surprised the enemy at 11 A.M., put-

*Sphinxhaven lies a few miles north of the German border.

ting him to flight and capturing two maxim guns. The main body following later met the main body of the enemy reformed, and fought a stiff fight for two hours, when the enemy retired in disorder. Their casualties were 130, whereas those of the British were only 63. This engagement left Nyassaland free for the rest of the war.

The border skirmishes, which alone marked the later operations in Nyassaland, were also the fate of Rhodesia. Kituta, at the Rhodesian end of Tanganyika, was sacked in September; and a few months later Major J. J.

Troops moving along a narrow forest track in Nyassaland. (*Wire Service*)

O'Sullevan, with the 2nd Mobile Column of Rhodesian Police, was ordered from the Caprivi territory of German South-West Africa to the eastern front. The marching of this body of troops was remarkable. In twenty days they had crossed the 430 miles, despite the heavy rains, swamps, and swollen rivers. Arrived at his destination. Major O'Sullevan was given a respite, for the rainy season was on, and the defeat at Karonga had had a wholesome influence. A fort was built at Saisi, near Abercorn, and in June 1915, the little force, strengthened by some Belgians, made some successful raids. Count Falkenstein thereupon made a vigorous attempt to deal with the force; but without success.

On July 24th the Germans, with 2,000 men, 12-pounder guns, and 10 machine-guns, made a more determined attempt upon

Saisi. The garrison was outnumbered by almost 5 to 1; but they had strengthened their defences, and held out for ten days. Some of the days were waterless, for the Germans lay near the wells, and water supplies had to be brought by night in bottles. After four days and nights of fighting, the Germans asked O'Sullevan to surrender. He refused and the fighting became fiercer. In spite of the Europeans being in the large majority among the assailants, they could not get the Arabs to charge. At length the enemy's food gave out; but the defenders were in the same state, and it was therefore with profound relief they watched the Germans withdraw. A Belgian battalion relieved O'Sullevan a few days later. A few months after the siege a fruitless attempt to march on Saisi was checked, and towards the end of the year Brigadier-General Edward Northey arrived to take command of the increased forces in Rhodesia and Nyassaland.

General Tighe pushed on his preparations towards the end of the year, and his force was largely increased. General Sir Horace Smith-Dorrien was appointed to command the force in December, but while on his way to Mombasa he was taken ill and forced to resign. General Smuts, who had already refused the command once, now, on a further appeal, accepted. He reached Mombasa on February 19th, and in a fortnight commenced to advance.

GENERAL SMUTS' CAMPAIGN

When General Smuts took over the command the German force was estimated at 16,000 strong, 2,000 being Europeans. It was well armed, and had 60 guns* and 80 machine-guns. At Taveta, in British territory, the enemy had established an entrenched camp with tentacles stretching some 10 miles north and south, and outposts at Serengeti and Mbuyuni—13 and 17 miles respectively to

*The *Konigsberg* provided a number of these, including ten of 4.1-inch calibre.

General Jan Christiaan Smuts (1870–1950) led South African forces against German South-West Africa and then commanded all British forces during the campaign against German East Africa. (*Library of Congress*)

the east. Still farther east was another garrison on British territory, and there was a considerable force near the coast which periodically raided the railway.

The plan which General Tighe had formed was to occupy the Kilimanjaro region by a converging advance from Longido and Mbuyuni, and to this General Smuts adhered in the main. Major-General Stewart, with the 1st Division, was to cross the 35 miles of waterless bush between Longido and the Nanjuki River, and then to march round the south-western slopes of Kilimanjaro to Boma-Jangombe, and thence to Moschi and Kahe. The force from Mbuyuni was to clear the Taveta position and thence advance to Kahe. By March 4th all arrangements had been made. A pipe-line had been laid, and with the help of storage tanks the watering of the force at Mbuyuni was carried out without a hitch, in spite of the damage inflicted by a German raid on the line east of Mbuyuni. The 1st Division had occupied Longido in January. Mbuyuni and Serengeti had been occupied a little later by the 2nd Division, under Brigadier-General Malleson, and the position at Salaita had been reconnoitred in force at the beginning of February.

General Stewart began his advance towards the rear of Kilimanjaro on March 5th, and on the afternoon of the following day the advance troops were at Nagasseni Hill. The following day

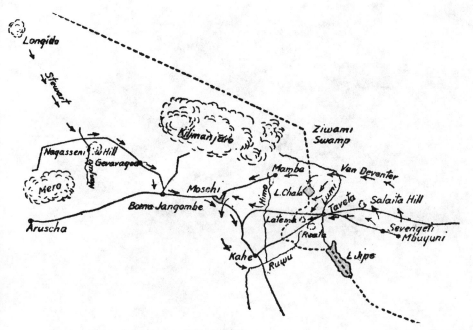

General Smuts' Campaign, March 1915.

the main force had come up, and on the 8th it moved to Geraragua. Two days later the mounted troops were engaged by a small force of the enemy, and suffered 13 casualties. The British force had left the main road, as it was found impossible for wheeled traffic; but, advancing on the west of it, reached Boma-Jangombe on the 13th. It had thus crossed the difficult country between Meru and Kilimanjaro, and lay south of the latter, not far from Moschi.

Meanwhile, the main forces had been engaged in the Taveta region, which lay in the eastern shadow of the snow-capped Kilimanjaro. General Smuts had intentionally given General Stewart two days' start for the larger outflanking scheme, and only in the evening of the 7th was Brigadier-General Van Deventer's force set in motion. Van Deventer, who had fought so brilliantly in German South-West Africa, was in command of the 1st South

German and Askari troops on patrol in East Africa (*Deutsche Kolonialgesellschaff Bibliothek*)

African Mounted Brigade (at Mbuyuni) and the 3rd South African Infantry Brigade (at Serengeti), and his role was to outflank the difficult Taveta position by seizing the high ground about Lake Chala, while the 2nd Division, under General Tighe, advanced towards Salaita Hill and entrenched themselves in preparation for attack. Smuts was following the tactics of the campaign in German South-West Africa, avoiding frontal attacks on prepared positions and compelling their evacuation by flank assaults.

Early in the morning of March 8th, Van Deventer's force was on the Lumi River, and forced the enemy to retreat by a converging movement from north, west, east, and south. Part of the German force was cut off, and this detachment, while mounted troops were pursuing the main body to Taveta, attacked the infantry, who were guarding the river-crossing, but was beaten off. On the following day Van Deventer compelled the evacuation of Taveta by cutting the road to Moschi on the west, and he sent troops to the river bridge, east of Taveta. It was owing to these operations that the

South African and East Asian troops rest after debarking from their transport to East Africa. (*Illustrated War News*)

strong Salaita position was evacuated before the 2nd Division advanced to the attack on the afternoon of the 9th. The enemy had been surprised; but, realising the gravity of his reverse, he determined to retake Taveta. The following day the town was seized in the face of a large force of the enemy, who was approaching to reoccupy it.

THE BATTLE OF LATEMA-REATA NEK

On March 11th, 1915, Van Deventer's force was stretched between Mamba and the strongly defended position at the Latema-Reata Nek. His right, at Mamba, was thus northward of the main body of the enemy, who was falling back along the Taveta-Moschi road, while his left was approaching the southern line of retreat by the road between the Latema and Reata Hills to Kahe. The nek was a position of considerable strength; but, since the road and railway to Kahe ran through it, General Smuts saw that he must take it before his advance could proceed from Taveta.

General Malleson, who was ordered to undertake the operation, decided to attack the Latema spur, which commands the nek from the north; and one of the fiercest engagements of the campaign developed on this hill. The 130th Baluchis and the 3rd K.A.R., on approaching the bush-clad slopes, found themselves under heavy rifle and machine-gun fire. After five hours' fighting little headway had been made, and General Malleson was too unwell to carry on. General Tighe, who assumed the immediate command with reinforcements, ordered another advance; but though the troops went forward, they failed to carry the ridge, and lost heavily.

It was then resolved to make a night attack with fresh troops; but by the time the positions had been almost won the attacking bodies had so diminished, owing to concentrated machine-gun fire, that it was impossible to proceed. And it was impossible to co-ordinate the movements during the night. The order was therefore given to fall back and await the effect of Van Deventer's movement towards the rear of the position. While the retirement was in progress it was found that the enemy was in full retreat. The ridge was promptly seized and the retreating enemy shelled as he threaded his way through the dense tropical forest beyond. The British sustained 270 casualties in this engagement. But the position was of the utmost importance, and the enemy suffered heavily and left much material behind.

THE ADVANCE ON KAHE

General Van Deventer advanced eastward from Mamba and along the Taveta-Moschi road, and on March 13th occupied Moschi unopposed. He was joined there on the following day by General Stewart's force from Boma-Jangombe. The enemy had fallen back towards Kahe. A few days were given to reorganisation and reconnoitring before the next forward movement. On the 18th a general

Men of the King's African Rifles (K.A.R.) encounter a hostile patrol in the jungle and prepare to return fire. (*Wire Service*)

advance began towards the Ruwu River, and the troops marched in three columns astride the Himo River. Two days later Van Deventer left Moschi with mounted troops to cross the Pangani and take Kahe in the rear. On the 21st he seized Kahe Station and Kahe Hill, which, lying to the rear of the Ruwu, commanded the position. The importance of the position was so obvious that it was subjected to several counter-attacks, but was firmly held.

General Stewart, advancing down the main road to Kahe, was separated by dense bush from Van Deventer, and did not know of his capture of Kahe Station. He came upon the main enemy position covered by two branching rivers. The troops on his left were held up by dense bush, and all his attempts to advance merely caused further casualties to his heroic troops. But during the night of the 21st the enemy retired across the Ruwu, and since Aruscha, south of Meru, had also been occupied, the conquest of the Kilimanjaro-Meru area, "probably the richest and most desirable district of German East Africa," was complete.

The railway had been laid (at the astounding rate of a mile a day) through Salaita, Taveta, and the Latema Nek, and the wet season found things ready for the next advance. The operation thus completed was the first unmistakable British success in the campaign, and it was largely determined by the preparations made before the arrival of General Smuts.

The Advance To The Railway

The troops were now reorganised. Indian and other British troops were to form one division, and the other two were formed of one mounted and one infantry brigade of troops from the Union of South Africa. The 1st Division (Major-General Hoskins) comprised the 1st East African Brigade (Brigadier-General Sheppard) and the 2nd East African Brigade (Brigadier-General J. H. Hannyngton). The 2nd Division (Major-General J. Van Deventer) comprised the 1st South African Mounted Brigade (Brigadier-General Manie Botha) and the 3rd South African Infantry Brigade (Brigadier-General C. A. L. Berrange). The 3rd Division (Major-General Coen Brits) comprised the 2nd South African Mounted Brigade (Brigadier-General B. Enslin) and the 2nd South African Infantry Brigade (Brigadier-General P. S. Beves).

General Smuts determined to strike into the interior of the colony with the 2nd Division, under Van Deventer. The line of advance offered many advantages. It was clearly not expected, since the main force of the enemy had retired along the Tanga Railway, where he had fortified positions in the Pare and Usambara mountains. He would be compelled to withdraw a considerable part of his force to deal with Van Deventer's advance, and the clearing of the Tanga district would thus be facilitated.

On April 1st the bulk of Van Deventer's force was concentrated at Aruscha, and two days later three regiments of South African

An Indian cavalry patrol reconnoitering for German movements in the East African brushland. (*Wire Service*)

Horse surrounded Lolkissale, 35 miles to the south. The enemy was strongly posted on a hill, the springs on which were the only water supply in the neighbourhood. A vigorous battle developed, and lasted two whole days; but on the 6th the enemy force of 421 men, with a considerable number of bearers, surrendered.

From information gained in captured documents, it was seen that reinforcements could not reach Kondoa Irangi for some weeks, and it was resolved to advance upon that settlement at once. The troops were accordingly sent forward, clearing the country east and west of the main line of advance, and on May 17th they came into contact with the enemy four miles north of Kondoa Irangi. There a fierce engagement took place for nearly 30 hours; but by noon of the 19th the enemy's resistance was broken and the British occupied Kondoa Irangi. They had inflicted heavy loss upon the enemy, but had suffered no casualties themselves.

This bold swoop of some 200 miles from Moschi in four weeks—one of the most brilliant episodes in the campaign—had greatly exhausted the horses. Many had died on the way, and the troops also were worn out with ceaseless marching and fighting. General Smuts therefore ordered the force to concentrate at Kondoa Irangi, sending patrols towards the Central Railway and eastwards towards Handeni.

In the highland where Van Deventer now stood he became isolated by the violence of the torrential rains which filled the valleys between Kondoa and Moschi. Local supplies of meat and Kafir corn, with occasional stores brought from Lolkissale—120 miles distant—by trains of bearers, were the only support of the little force. In their fatigued condition the underfeeding made many an easy prey to malaria.

THE BATTLE OF KONDOA IRANGI

The enemy meanwhile had skilfully transferred a large force from Usambara by the Central Railway; and on May 7th he advanced, some 4,000 strong, against Van Deventer's position. The British could muster barely 3,000 rifles, and Van Deventer gradually withdrew before the enemy until on the 9th his force lay on a defensive position of some five miles perimeter about Kondoa Irangi village. The main assault began about 7.30 P.M., and for eight hours continued with little cessation.

Four desperate attacks were made; but the enemy was stopped dead at the British positions, and at 3.15 A.M. withdrew, leaving 61 dead on the ground. The British losses were 2 officers and 4 other ranks killed, and 18 wounded. The enemy was under the personal command of Colonel von Lettow-Vorbeck, the commander-in-chief, and with his defeat perished the last hope of successful resistance to any large portion of the British troops. It was the first and last attempt at a considerable offensive, and as it had failed when all the odds were in its favour, the Germans recognised that there was nothing to be hoped from such tactics. Von Lettow-Vorbeck continued to occupy positions near Kondoa throughout May and the greater part of June, and the sickness of the British troops and weakness of communications made it impossible for Van Deventer to assume the offensive.

TOWARD THE END OF THE SECOND WEEK IN MAY, the rains having somewhat abated, General Smuts determined to take advantage of the enemy concentration about Kondoa to clear the Usambara district. His plan was to move eastwards until he reached a point opposite Handeni, and then to swing southwards and march towards the Central Railway in a line parallel to that of Van Deventer's advance. The enemy held the Pare and Usambara mountains and the railway below them, and had outposts on the river Pangani, which runs roughly parallel to the line of the railway. It was along the railway the enemy expected the British to advance, and positions had been strongly fortified.

The British main column (Sheppard's and Beves' brigades), however, moved along the northern bank of the Pangani in advance of a smaller force (Hannyngton's brigade) moving along the railway; and a third column (Lieutenant-Colonel Fitzgerald's battalion 3rd K.A.R.) was to thread the Pares through the Ngulu gap and join the central column at Same Pass. The Pangani advance was in the nature of a turning movement, and it achieved wonderful success.

On May 26th, Colonel Fitzgerald, after a march marked by little incident, joined Hannyngton's force near Same Station. Hannyngton was now ordered to cross the Same Pass, and on May 31st he had successfully accomplished this task, turning the intervening positions on the railway and reaching Mkomanzi Road Bridge. Nowhere did the troops meet with any serious resistance, and when they reached Mombo and found the enemy following the trolley line to Handeni, it became clear that the Germans did not intend to make a serious stand in the Usambara. The British had in ten days covered 130 miles of trackless country, and their skilful dispositions had made the enemy position hopeless.

General Smuts now determined to cross the Pangani with his main column and leave Hannyngton to clear the Usambara. While the bridge over the river was being repaired, General Smuts visited Kondoa, and on his return on June 7th the troops were across the river, and had moved 30 miles along the southern bank. General Sheppard marched swiftly towards Handeni, which he occupied on the 19th; and on the following day he was joined by Hannyngton, who had entered Wilhemstal on the 12th and cleared the railway to Korogwe three days later.

Without any pause, the enemy was pursued to the river Lukigura, General Hoskins crossing by night north of the German positions. The following day the enemy, attacked on three sides, was defeated with considerable loss, and fell back on strong positions in the Nguru Mountains. General Smuts, seeing the strength of the enemy position, determined to rest and refit his troops. They had marched more than 200 miles in the last month over difficult country, and the transport difficulties had been such that they could only secure half rations for some time. Lack of water, added to these trials, resulted in malaria making great headway.

THE EASTERN USAMBARA HAD BEEN LEFT TO ITSELF. General Smuts had hoped that the development of operations elsewhere would cause the enemy to retreat. Even if they chose to hold to their positions, he knew that he was directly ensuring their defeat by dealing more vigorously with the main force of the enemy. On June 16th he set small forces in motion to clear up the situation there; and to such good purpose did they act that in two months not only Eastern Usambara but the coast region down to Bagamoyo had been cleared. In these operations General Smuts made use of converging columns, one of these being frequently the Navy.

The enemy was over the British border when the operations commenced; but he was rapidly driven back. Tanga was occupied on July 7th, and the railway and district up to Korogwe were cleared. Pangani was taken by the Navy, and the enemy was caught at Manga, beaten, and driven to Mandera, on the Wami River. The Navy continued to clear the coast, and on August 15th brilliantly captured Bagamoyo, where the land force concentrated.

The Opening of the Belgian Campaign

Meanwhile, satisfactory arrangements having been made with General Tombeur, commanding the Belgian forces, the enemy had been cleared out of the north-western corner of the colony and was in full retreat upon the Central Railway. Brigadier-General Sir Charles Crewe co-operated with General Tombeur, and the Belgian base was removed to a point on Lake Victoria, the British making themselves responsible for transport and supply to this base. A column moved into British territory to march southward on Kigali, the capital of the rich enemy province of Ruanda.

Colonel Molitor arrived in Uganda at the end of April, and on the last day of the month one of his columns was well over the German borders. A week later it was in Kigali. The German forces to the west and east were thus outflanked, and General Tombeur was enabled to push forward other columns from north and south of Lake Kivu. The latter (Olsen's brigade) entered Usumbura. A regiment of Molitor's column had already occupied Nyanza, and this opened up another route for the left wing of Olsen's column. This regiment was heavily engaged on the Akanjaru, but forced the enemy to retreat, and thence marched south upon Gitega, which the right-wing regiment was also approaching from the west. Gitega occupied, the left wing marched direct for Tabora, the right marching south to clear the western shores of Tanganyika to the terminus of the Central Railway.

Colonel Molitor's column had turned eastward, and was now marching towards Lake Victoria; and, as he approached it, the British troops began to clear the Kagera region. In the middle of June Sir Charles Crewe took command of the British forces in this area. Ukerewe Island, Lake Victoria, had already been seized by a little force, assisted by a naval flotilla, and, lying just north of the important German station of Mwansa, it afforded a useful base for operations against the town. Two columns were employed for these operations; one landed northeast of the town and another due east. The latter threatened the rear of the Mwansa garrison, and the town was evacuated on July 14th. The British, in co-operation with Colonel Molitor's column, had already cleared the western side of Lake Victoria, and thus at this date the area north of a line from the lake to Tanganyika was completely free of the enemy.

The result had only been obtained by the skilful cooperation of the Allied forces. There were few engagements, since the Allied columns invariably turned the enemy positions. Olsen's left wing had established contact with Molitor's right, and by the end of July the troops who had been devoted to the defence of the western shores of Tanganyika became available for the advance on Tabora, owing to the destruction of the German naval units on the lake.

Van Deventer Cuts the Railway

Van Deventer had meanwhile recommenced his aggressive tactics. The enemy had begun to appreciate the precariousness of his position. The British force at the foot of the Nguru Mountains was on the flank of the enemy about Kondoa Irangi, and troops from the latter were taken to strengthen the Nguru army. At the end of June, Van Deventer cleared the enemy from his line of advance and set about active preparations for a swift descent upon the Central Railway.

At the beginning of August a small column occupied Singida on the right flank of his advance. But by this time a column of the same size, under Colonel H. J. Fitzpatrick, had occupied Saranda on the Central Railway and Kilimatinde, 7 miles south of it on the main central road. Van Deventer's main column moved upon Dodoma. His way of advance was dictated by the water-holes; and these were occupied by the enemy. So the force was divided into two columns under Brigadier-General Manie Botha and Brigadier-General Berrangé. The latter met with some resistance; but his armoured motor battery counterbalanced the strong enemy entrenchments, and Dodoma was entered on July 29th. General Manie Botha had to retire to South Africa at this point, and General Nussey (Van Deventer's former Chief of Staff) took command of the column, which a day later occupied Kikombi Station. The British had thus 100 miles of the Central Railway in their hands.

A week later Van Deventer had concentrated his force at Nyangalo, on the main road to Mpapua. In the second week of August the position was one of great interest. All the coast to Bagamoyo had been cleared, the Central Railway was occupied for 100 miles, the Belgian and British forces were well south of Lake Victoria, and General Northey's force from Nyassaland had taken Malangali, after a "brilliant little action," and was preparing to move on Iringa—70 miles north-east.

In between the British force below Handeni and Van Deventer's force lay the block of the Nguru Mountains, which commanded the Central Railway and main road. In the mountains and across the main road, towards the west, were some 3,000 enemy troops skilfully entrenched with heavy and light artillery. To advance along the road would be to leave the enemy to the north in a position to fall upon the British communications. Hence safety required that the formidable mountain position should be attacked. The main valley, the Mdjongo, was strongly held by the enemy, who also held positions to the north-east. The 1st Division was directed to carry these positions and advance along the valley, while the 3rd Division turned into a tributary valley towards the west, which emerged from the mountains at Turiani, below the Mhonda Mission.

General Enslin's (2nd Division) mounted brigade entered the mountains on August 5th, and occupied Mhonda three days later. It had been intended to send General Beves' brigade after it; but as wheeled traffic could not follow the track, these troops joined General Hannyngton at Matomondo, in the Mjongo Valley. Thus it happened that Enslin found himself with the key positions in his hands through which the enemy must retreat, but without sufficient troops to hold them.

At Matomondo a fierce battle was fought on August 10th and 11th; but the enemy was driven off with great loss, and when, on the latter day, General Sheppard advanced on the east of Matomondo, the enemy had fled. He followed him rapidly, crossed the Wami, and reached the crossing at Dakava as Enslin arrived nearly opposite on the northern bank. Here a heavy battle was fought; but Enslin could not cross the wide and deep river to help Sheppard, who was unable to make any headway. The British lost 120 men in this action, but the enemy had lost more heavily; and when Enslin crossed the river higher up they retired rapidly to the south.

A caravan making its way along the hills of East Africa. Soon after this photograph was taken the column was attacked by a German force. The African, Indian, and British soldiers successfully repulsed the enemy and continued their mission. (*Wire Service*)

THE ATTEMPT TO SURROUND MOROGORO

Van Deventer, during the clearing of the Nguru Mountains, was marching and fighting his way to Mpapawa, which he entered on August 12th, The way lay through dense bush, where ambushes could not be located until they were experienced. He stormed entrenched positions, went forward again into further ambushes against other entrenchments, and so took his weary men to Kilossa on August 22nd. All the men were underfed, all had to go long hours without water or rest; yet even in such conditions they still went forward, when their commander ordered them, in obedience to General Smuts's request.

The enemy had concentrated at Uleia. They were driven out on August 26th, and a fortnight later the troops occupied Kidodi, on the river Ruaha. On their way there they had to pass carefully-entrenched mountain positions. Yet there were few casualties, the troops being directed towards the flanks of the positions which were evacuated under the threat of being taken from the rear.

General Smuts meanwhile had made another attempt to force the enemy to accept battle by attempting to pen him into Morogoro. The Uluguru Mountains lie south of the town, and Smuts, having blocked the retreat to the west, sent columns to hold the eastern and western flanks. Enslin was ordered to move south, and, crossing the Central Railway west of Morogoro, he occupied Mlali, on the western road to Kissaki, on August 24th. He was thus but 15 miles from Morogoro and on the south-west. Van Deventer was ordered to move on Kidodi to block the road to Mahenge, and reached his objective, as we have seen, on September 10th. Another force was thrown across the Wami River to the east, and after an heroic march through dense bush in tropical weather, worked round the eastern flank of the Uluguru Hills. But the German commander had realised his peril, and had fallen back towards Mahenge by a southern track through the hills of which the British command had no knowledge. Morogoro was occupied on August 26th, but the British found that the enemy had again escaped.

The British advanced along the eastern slopes constantly in touch with strong German rearguards. The mountain positions and dense bush—higher than a tall man—offered every chance to the enemy; and at one place the mountain side had to be blasted away to form a road for the transport. At another place, where the road crosses one of the spurs of the mountains, which ends with a precipitous face, a pass was cut through the spur and down the face by the technical corps—"a notable engineering feat," as General Smuts justly remarks. Actions were fought daily and prisoners taken.

At Dutumi, 18 miles east of Kissaki, Hannyngton's brigade, which was leading the advance, fought a pitched battle for several days before succeeding in driving the enemy south of the Mgeta

River. The western columns in their advance found every evidence, in abandoned munition heaps and guns, that the enemy had meant to make a prolonged stand, but for the bewildering rapidity of the British movements through the mountains. General Brits reached Kissaki by the elephant track which Burton and Speke had followed into the interior in 1857.*

In the difficult terrain an unsuccessful action was fought against Kissaki on September 7th. General Beves, on one side of the Mgeta, could give no help to Enslin, who was attacked on the other by superior forces; and both had to retire. To make matters worse, General Nussey, unaware of what had happened, arrived before Kissaki the following morning, and fought a stubborn action against superior forces until he was bidden to retire by General Brits, who was held off by the bush from assisting his subordinate. At the end of the second week of September, Dutumi fell, and Kissaki, threatened by General Enslin from the north-east, was evacuated. In it was found the enemy's hospital full of sick; but the stores had all been removed. The enemy fell back to the Mgeta River and astride the road from Kissaki to the Rufigi; and the British were forced to rest and refit their troops.

Dar-es-Salaam fell on September 3rd. Two columns converged on it from the land side, and the Navy co-operated from the sea. General Smuts now arranged for all the important points on the coast to be occupied, and by the third week in September this operation had been carried out. The ports were occupied as far as the Portuguese border, and the German force was finally cut off from the coast.

---

*Richard Burton and John Speke were the first Europeans to reach Lake Tanganyika. Speke also found a second lake he named Lake Victoria.

Capture of Tabora

Meanwhile, the Belgian force lying north of the western end of the Central Railway had developed their operations with skill and energy. It was arranged that Sir Charles Crewe and General Tombeur should start together down the two main roads to Tabora. Their immediate destinations were St. Michael and Iwingo. General Crewe reached Iwingo, on the western road, on August 7th, but Colonel Molitor did not arrive at St. Michael until five days later; and, as the enemy lay entrenched to the south, he had to renew his supplies of ammunition and stores before he could proceed. Olsen's column was meanwhile moving forward towards Tabora from the west; and the enemy was engaged west and south-west of Tabora on September 1st and 2nd. Moulaert was marching thither south of the railway, and Colonel Molitor recommenced his advance from St. Michael.

The rapidity of Molitor's movements may be gathered from the fact that all the columns reached the outer defences of Tabora simultaneously on September 7th. The enemy had fallen back to avoid the converging columns, which had maintained communication with each other though over 100 miles apart. Molitor found his advance checked at Mambali, due north of Tabora; Olsen was engaged at Usoke to the west; and Moulaert was giving battle to the south, at Sikonge. Each of these places was about 30 miles distant from Tabora, and about these positions General Wahle held off the Belgian columns for eleven days. He had much heavy artillery, and the tide of battle swayed until the 18th, when the German defeat was complete.

Olsen and Molitor entered Tabora on the following day, and a week later Crewe occupied Igalulu, on the railway, east of Tabora. The enemy had suffered heavily. The dead bodies of 50 Europeans and 300 black soldiers were found on the field, and 100 European

Bearers wading through the shallows of Lake Bangweulu, Rhodesia [Zambia], while carrying supplies to support an expedition against the Germans. David Livingstone died near here in 1873. (*Wire Service*)

officers and non-commissioned officers and numerous native soldiers were taken prisoners, with much material. On entering the town, the Belgians were able to liberate 189 Europeans of allied nations who had been interned. Belgium by this victory rounded off her occupation of a territory more than six times her own area.

THE RETREAT TO MAHENGE

The enemy fell back once more, one column, under Wahle, marching eastward along the railway, and then south to the Itumba Mountains, while another, under Max Wintgens, retired southwards through Sikonge. Towards the end of October both columns were approaching the Great Ruaha River north and west respectively of Iringa.

General Northey had pushed his column towards the north-west to intercept this force and prevent its junction with the main German army. He occupied Lupembe a week after Molitor entered

St. Michael, and ten days later entered Iringa. He would have occupied Iringa earlier but that General Smuts advised him to slow down while the line of the enemy's retreat was uncertain.

The role of the Lupembe column was to watch the Ruhuje River and the enemy force at Mahenge, while the column at Iringa, which was in touch with Van Deventer, had the task of dealing with Wahle's force from Tabora. On October 19th this force came into contact with Northey's column south of Iringa, and the Mahenge troops assumed the offensive with the object of assisting Wahle to break through Northey's line. The enemy was defeated at Iringa and thrown back over the Ruhuje, losing 200 killed and wounded, 82 prisoners, and considerable material.

Another enemy detachment, after an initial success at Mgominyi, was driven off from Malangali. The German force then divided into two columns, one of which invested Lupembe until it was dispersed by British columns. The remainder was driven into Itembule Mission and forced to surrender on November 26th. This success gave Northey 7 officers, 47 other Europeans, and 449 native troops, and a 10.5cm howitzer with ammunition and 3 machine-guns. There were also killed or otherwise accounted for (in addition to those disposed of or removed by the enemy) 71 Germans and 370 native soldiers. The remnants of Wahle's force, having lost the bulk of its artillery and machine-guns and over 50 percent of its original strength, succeeded in effecting a junction with the main German body on the Mahenge plateau. They could never have escaped but for the difficulties of provisioning a sufficient body of troops to operate against them.

WITHDRAWAL OF NON-NATIVE TROOPS

Meanwhile, General Smuts had effected a complete reorganisation of his force. As the army marched south it soon became obvious that the imported European troops were unfit for the conditions of the campaign. Two-thirds of the British force were troops who came fresh to this trying country, whereas not more than an eighth of the German force were Europeans, and only a small number of these were not acclimatised by long residence in the country. The vast tsetse-haunted belts of country had speedily accounted for the bulk of the horses. In six weeks a mounted force of 1,000 men lost well over 90 percent of their mounts. Malaria and dysentery wrought havoc among the men, and those who escaped were worn out with the additional labour which fell to their share owing to so many of their comrades being sick. During the last three months of 1915 the bulk of the non-native troops—some 12,000 men—were accordingly evacuated, their place being taken by new battalions of the King's African Rifles, trained on the spot, and the Nigerian force of Brigadier-General Cunliffe, which landed at Dar-es-Salaam in December. The whole army was once more split into two divisions. One of these, under General Hoskins, occupied the east and centre, while the other, under Van Deventer, operated on the west. Northey's force co-operated with Van Deventer's division, and occupied the south-west of the vast irregular arc which the British had thrown about the enemy.

The whole of the arc could not be held in equal strength throughout its extent, and the position offered chances to an active enemy. The Germans were not slow to seize their opportunity, and, being on interior lines, were able to concentrate against the weaker links of the chain. For some little time Northey was cut off from his force in Iringa, and Van Deventer assumed command of the column there. In December the enemy made a determined attempt to surround the detachments at Kibata; but he was driven off, and towards the end of the month a concerted British offensive was resumed.

The enemy about this time lay within a rough arc resting on the Portuguese frontier, on the east not far from the coast and on the west near Lake Nyassa. Its northern sector jutted north across the Rufigi on the east and the Kilimbero on the north-west. General Smuts had resolved to deliver his main blow in the Rufigi area. His plan was to cross the Rufigi River and, placing a strong detachment on the left flank and rear of the force lying 30 miles to the north on the Mgeta, cut it off and compel it to choose between surrender or annihilation. General Beves was sent to cross the Rufigi on the west, while the rest of his command north of the Mgeta held the enemy there.

On the first day of the New Year the Nigerian Brigade began the holding attack, while columns worked round the enemy flanks; but the enemy fell back in the night, and the troops came up with them three days later, 20 miles south of the Mgeta. The day before Beves had crossed the Rufigi, and entrenched a position.

Again the enemy refused battle; but he was harassed in his retirement by the pursuing troops, and it was in this engagement that Captain Selous fell at the head of his company of Royal Fusiliers. The enemy retired across the Rufigi, and part of Hannyngton's force from Kilwa, moving north to threaten his retreat, occupied Mohoro on January 16th. Four days later General Smuts handed over the command to General Hoskins, and left to attend the Imperial Conference. He had broken the back of the enemy's resistance in his campaign, though the fighting was still to drag on for many months.

The German strength had fallen to about 1,100 whites and 7,300 Askaris. A strong detachment still lay north of Mpanganya opposing the advance of a British column under Colonel Burns.

The rest of the German Eastern force held part of the southern bank of the Rufigi, and lay in the Kitschi Hills. Beves was at Makalinso. Northey, in the west, had forced the enemy east of the Ruhuje River, and pressed them back from Lake Nyassa to Kitanda and Likuju, at which place 40 Germans and 200 Askaris were compelled to surrender on January 24th.

Meanwhile, with the object of clearing the Rufigi delta. Colonel Burns's column was pressed forward from the north, while the column from Mohoro moved towards the west. The Navy supported by clearing the channels of the river. On January 21st, Utete (near Mpanganya) was occupied by the Mohoro column; and the northern bank of the river was practically clear by the beginning of February.

But before this the whole situation had been changed by the early onset of the heaviest rainy season for nine years. In a short time the character of the campaign was revolutionised. In the southern area the roads, skilfully laid for motor transport, could only be used by porters marching waist deep in water. In the centre, flat-bottomed boats had to be prepared to convey supplies, while in the Rufigi Valley patrol work had to be carried out for some time in canoes, and the men found themselves making fast to the roofs of houses which had lately formed their quarters. Sickness broke out in the coastal area, malaria carrying off the white troops, while pneumonia made headway even among the African natives.

In the south-west, the rains were not so heavy, and the several enemy columns in that area at length formed two bodies. One of these, under Major Kraut, struck southward, and, though hotly pursued, crossed the Portuguese frontier and raided the colony for food. The other body, under Major Wintgens, moved westwards. A British detachment reconnoitering from Tandala to the south-west was heavily attacked by the German troops and fell back under

cover of darkness. Wintgens then invested Tandala until a relief column under Colonel Murray arrived on February 22nd, when he
marched northward. He had with him some 600 men, one-tenth
being whites; and although he was followed with the greatest rapidity he eluded the detachments sent after him, passed Lake Rukwa,
and marched northwards towards Tabora. Time after time he
seemed on the verge of capture; but contrived to escape, and on
April 5th reached Kitunda Mission, where he was able to replenish
his supplies. A column was dispatched to Tabora to head him off;
another advanced from the southern end of Tanganyika. A Belgian
column was moving against him from the Central Railway, and
Wintgens, suffering from malaria, surrendered to its commander,
Major Bataille, 60 miles south of Tabora, on May 22nd; but the
bulk of his force—Askaris from the Mwanza—crossed the railway
and made for home. They were hunted hither and thither until they
were finally captured in September by the British, over 400 miles
from where they had set out.

THE CAPTURE OF MAHENGE

But before this episode was concluded General Hoskins had carried
out a reorganisation of the forces and handed over the command to
General Van Deventer. About the beginning of May the German
forces were found to be withdrawing to the Matondu Valley, and
when General Van Deventer took command, on May 30th, the
rainy season had ended, and a new problem confronted him. He
concentrated his main force at Kilwa, and in June began a simulta-
neous advance from this port and from Lindi, at the mouth of the
Lukuledi. General von Lettow-Vorbeck fell back slowly, fighting
rearguard actions, until he reached Narongombe, 33 miles south-
west of Kilwa, where he gave battle on a strong position covering the
routes to the south. On July 19th a fierce struggle raged throughout

British Army Transport section on the road to the East African front. Transport of supplies was difficult in the hilly jungle terrain of East Africa and the numerous rivers and streams added to the logistics problems. (*Wire Service*)

the day. Both sides suffered heavily; but the Germans fell back once more to the Mbemkurru Valley.

At Mahungo, on the Mbemkurru, the Germans had established an important base. A pause followed the battle at Narongombe; but in September the offensive was resumed, and on the 28th a Kilwa column and a detachment from Kiswere converged on Mahungo and captured it. The enemy was driven across the river and was followed to the Lukuledi Valley. The Lindi force had been held up by the severe local rains during July and August; but it now resumed the offensive and marched down the river upon Nyangao as one of the Kilwa columns was approaching it from the north. On October 17th the town was captured at the very time that the western column of the Kilwa force was entering Lukuledi Mission, farther up the river. In the engagements which gave the British these two important centres the enemy lost 53 Europeans and 268 Askaris killed, and 241 Europeans and 677 Askaris surrendered. Von Lettow-Vorbeck's force fell back to the south, much weaker and ill-supplied, to the mountainous region below the Lukuledi.

Meanwhile, Belgian columns had been concentrated upon the railway and sent towards Mahenge. They were ably directed by Colonel Huighe, and the first column moving south from Dodoma, under Commandant Hubert, reached Iringa, and fought there with the British until it had effected a junction at Fakaras with the second column, under Major Bataille, from Kilossa, on August 29th. The British then left the Belgian troops, who crossed the Kilimbero, forced their way through the swamps south of the river, fought for a week in the hills beyond the swamps, and then came up with an enemy force of 2,000 men under Colonel Theodor Tafel, lying entrenched west of Mahenge.

By this time one of Northey's columns was approaching this centre after the siege of Mpepo. The bulk of the garrison had escaped and broken up into small parties, which made for Mahenge.

The Belgians fought a heavy battle with the enemy west of Mahenge. Columns were sent out east and west to envelop the Germans; but they were not strong enough, and when the Belgians entered Mahenge on October 9, 1917, the bulk of the enemy had retired eastward on Mganjira.

THE LAST PHASE

The capture of Mahenge, with much war material, 109 Europeans, and 156 Askaris, marked the penultimate stage of the campaign. One of Northey's columns was but a few miles away when it fell to the Belgians. Another had advanced up the Luwegu to Mponda, 50 miles south of Mahenge, and fought its way up to Mganjira. A third column marched from Ssongea through Likuju to Liwale, which it entered on October 29th.

The enemy was virtually cut into two bodies: Tafel's force north of the Ssongea-Liwale road, and von Lettow's south of the Lukuledi. General Van Deventer attempted to make this division final by bringing a Belgian column, under Commandant Henrion, to Kilwa and sending it to Liwale. The last phase of the campaign began. Tafel, seeing his danger, made all haste to join his commander, who lay nearly 200 miles to the south-east. Until November 6th he had held off Northey's column; but then finding his area of movement circumscribed, he broke southward, and on November 15th was near Liwale. There he encountered the weak column of Colonel Shorthose, which had marched from the southern end of Lake Nyassa across the Rovuma through Tunduru—an incredible journey—to join hands with the column from Likuju. Tafel's force completely outnumbered the small body of King's African Rifles under Shorthose, and he was thus able to break through the British cordon and make for Nevala.

Meanwhile, Van Deventer moved forward against the main body of von Lettow's troops in the Lukuledi Valley on November 6th, and in a fortnight the enemy had been forced out of the hills into the valley beyond. Fierce engagements were fought on the 15th and

18th, as a result of which the enemy lost in captures alone 376 Germans and 1,100 Askaris, and his resistance was broken completely.

On November 21, 1917, the British entered Nevala, capturing 178 Germans; and von Lettow fled across the Portuguese border.

Just six days after, Tafel, in complete ignorance of what had befallen his chief, after a brilliant march reached Nevala, and was there forced to surrender, with 100 Germans and 1,212 Askaris, and 2,200 other natives. On December 1st, General Van Deventer was able to announce that reconnaissances had definitely established the fact that German East Africa was cleared of the enemy.

In the last four months of the campaign, 1,410 Europeans and 4,149 native soldiers, 11 guns, and 56 machine-guns were captured.

7

REVIEW OF THE CAMPAIGNS

I T HAS SOMETIMES BEEN THOUGHT THAT these campaigns in the German Colonies were not skilfully conducted because two of them were protracted. The impression seems to be prevalent that the more disorganised a country is, the easier it should be to conquer. The opposite is nearer the truth. In these vast stretches of country considerable bodies of men may even evade notice for weeks by avoiding frequented routes, whereas in a European country it would be difficult to escape notice for as many hours. And to deal with an active and well-led force it is necessary to employ great numbers of troops, and to keep great numbers of troops in the field it is necessary to have well-developed communications. With a highly developed system of communications a smaller invading force can be used. Failing such a system, greater numbers must be used, and they will go handicapped into battle because of the poverty of communications upon which their supply and munitions depend.

If we bear this in mind, and remember also that even after the successful campaigns of General Smuts the perimeter of the area in which the enemy lay was over 1,000 miles, we may gather a juster notion of the task which the Allies accomplished in the colonial campaigns. The country, too, was difficult. Much of the fighting took place in mountains. Frequently vast stretches of almost impenetrable bush had to be passed. Sometimes a way had to be cut through, and the clearances to which the unwary looked as a haven were often found to be swept with machine-guns or sown with landmines.

General Smuts spoke with high appreciation of the behaviour of his troops :

> Their work has been done under tropical conditions which not only produce bodily weariness and unfitness, but which create mental langour and depression, and finally appall the stoutest hearts. To march day by day, and week by week, through the African jungle or high grass, in which vision is limited to a few yards, in which danger always lurks near but seldom becomes visible, even when experienced, supplies a test to human nature often, in the long run, beyond human endurance.

The climate severely tried the constitutions of all the troops, malaria, dysentery, and pneumonia finding many victims.

> That the enemy had also to contend with sickness, and with sameness if not with scarcity of food, is certain, but in a minor degree, since his white men were more acclimatised to German East Africa and his native soldiers indigenous to the country. He had the advantage of falling back upon interior lines . . . and of his power of living on the country as he retired. This last was accentuated by the fact that whereas we are accustomed to take and pay for only what the villagers can spare, the Germans have no scruples

General Botha accepts the surrender of German forces and the control of their South-West African colony on July 8, 1915. (*Wire Service*)

about taking all. And after using men, women, and children as porters so far as they require, they send them back in a starving condition, thus increasing the difficulties of our advancing troops.*

Yet in this ensemble of difficulties the dominance of personality stands out the more remarkable. General Botha forced the pace to such an extent in South-West Africa that the German commander flatly refused to believe that there were troops in his rear—that, in fact, he was cornered. Botha would ride ahead in a motor-car with the smallest bodyguard. His staff complained to General Smuts of the risk. They were told not to allow their General to run such risks. General Smuts showed the same indifference to danger in East

*General Hoskins' dispatch.

Africa; and there can be no doubt that this c haracteristic of both men had a material effect on the response of the troops when they were asked to take risks and make sacrifices.

In campaigns which were forced like these we must attribute the success to the same quality which Moltke gave as the explanation of Napoleon's successful pursuit after Jena: *will*—the will to exact the persistent advance when the intellect has measured its necessity. But the achievements of Generals Smuts and Van Deventer in East Africa would not be justly appreciated without some realisation of the skill and courage of von Lettow's resistance and of the quality of his Askari troops. He got every ounce of advantage out of his positions, and he was only beaten by more masterful minds.

Index